Head Hunters

Hunting Safaris Around the Globe

New Zealand

Joshua Godfrey

Joshua Godfrey

Dedication

To my beloved daughters Bianca and Zafiro Godfrey,

This book is dedicated to you both with all my heart. Your love and support have been my inspiration throughout this journey, and I am eternally grateful for your unwavering encouragement.

May this book serve as a testament to the love and devotion I have for you both, and may it inspire you to follow your dreams, wherever they may lead.

With all my love,

Dad

Contents

Part 1: Hunting

Chapter 1

Hunting as a Hobby

When I started hunting, I got addicted to the thrill and adrenaline that accompanies it. With time, I started seeing the benefits of hunting and researching it. After traveling to several countries and hunting on different terrains, I decided to write a few books for hunting enthusiasts. This book focuses on New Zealand and is aimed at people looking to start hunting as a hobby or those who just want to experience hunting for the first time.

This book is informational and relives several of my hunting and traveling experiences. A few starting chapters discuss hunting information: history, methods, types, and gears. After that, I talked about the hunting experience in New Zealand and the most famous hunting locations. I mentioned a few big games on plains and the mountains and what small games people usually go for. Finally, I concluded the hunting section by discussing what to do after successfully hunting your game.

I also discussed fishing in New Zealand, as it is as famous as hunting, and the experience is worth it. I talked about the history, methods, basics, gear, and some skills that are necessary for a great fishing experience. I also talked about different types of fish and places to go fishing.

Hunting is instinctive and part of our genetic coding because, for early humans, hunting was necessary. The hunted animal provided food and clothing, along with materials for tools from bones and horns. Apart from the archaeological pieces of evidence, you can find hunting in the primitive societies in the present era, albeit with some innovative hunting strategies. Of course, the hunting methods and weapons vary due to different terrains, types of animals, and the environment. The hunting weapon evolved from spears, sticks, and stones to specially shaped clubs like the knobkerrie and the Australian boomerang. The early hunters started using camouflages to increase their chances of getting a catch and went on to invent noose, snares, traps, pits, and baits. Around ten thousand years ago, humans started using dogs to aid their hunts and incorporated horses around four thousand years ago. As the human's dependency on agriculture and livestock breeding increased, hunting became less famous for food but remained in fashion for protecting crops, herds, or flocks.

Hunting predates our nearest ancestors, the homo sapiens, and goes as early as when Homo erectus used to roam around (around two million years ago). Archeological evidence of stone tools and the use of spears give undisputed evidence of hunting as means for food. Even early human societies were divided into hunters and gatherers, and this classification is found in our closest species, the chimpanzees. The earliest stone spearheads were found in South Africa around five hundred thousand years ago.[1]

The hunting hypothesis is a popular theory that hunting influenced our ancestors to evolve and helped us, the homo sapiens, survive while the others went extinct. Our early ancestors started using stone tools and learned to control fire to aid hunting and preparing food. As hunting large animals like mammoths required a group effort, we also started interacting and working together, which led to social interaction. These social interactions are vital in developing language, culture, and mating behavior.[2]

Some Mesolithic hunting lifestyles (around ten thousand years ago) are still found in the Americas, Sub-Saharan Africa, and Siberia. Hunting was a vital part of a lot of pagan religious traditions, and even in the religions practiced today, we see a lot of famous hunters like Esau (brother of Jacob in Christian and Jewish faith), Artemis and Hercules (Greek Mythology), and Diana (Roman Mythology).

Hunting has evolved with time, and now it is mainly used as trophy hunting or hobby and is significantly strictly regulated everywhere. In Africa, safari hunting is a popular way of hunting

---

[1] Morin, M. (2012). Archives. Retrieved from
http://articles.latimes.com/2012/nov/16/science/la-sci-hafting-spears-20121116
[2] Buss, D. (2011). *The Handbook of evolutionary psychology.*

made famous by President Theodore Roosevelt and Ernest Hemingway. It is a week-long hunt involving camping, pursuing, and stalking big game. In India, hunting was only reserved for the royal families and British officers. They often used elephants for hunting, traveling with a large hunting party, and hunting dangerous predators like the Bengal tigers. England was famous for foxhunting and using hounds to aid in hunts. Many dog species were specially bred to help with hunting, like the Golden Retriever, Greyhounds and Spaniels.

Countries like Russia, Iran, Japan, and Trinidad and Tobago have a history of hunting as a sport which is still followed today. The Middle East usually prefers falcon hunting, spending hundreds of thousands of dollars on it. However, hunting in Australia started when they needed to cull certain invasive species and pests. Under strict observation, the government culls several animals like kangaroos, emus, wallabies, and sharks.

Hunting in the United States is older than when Christopher Columbus arrived. The Native Americans used to hunt large game animals like deer, caribou, moose, elk, buffalo, and bear, and some small game like rabbits, muskrat, and beavers. Aboriginals from the Great Plains used to hunt bison using bows and arrows, spears, tomahawks, snares, and traps. The United States strictly regulates hunting and specializes in migratory birds and endangered species. The big game animals that are hunted in the States are white-tailed deer, moose, elk, bear, caribou, bighorn sheep, boar, and bison. Rabbit, hare, squirrel, porcupine, skunk, armadillo, and ruffed grouse are part of small game quarries. There are furbearers like the red fox, beaver, pine marten, muskrat, bobcat, and coyote, which are part of the hunting game, and some predators like the cougar, wolf, and coyote are also hunted. Game birds include grouse, chukar, pheasant, quail, dove, and waterfowl, including duck, teal, geese, and swan.

Hunting isn't a one-sided affair, although the use of rifles and shotguns makes it advantageous for the hunter. Nowadays, hunters are obliged to follow fair chase principles, giving the game an excellent chance to escape. Fair chase makes the hunt ethical and makes the search worthwhile.

President Teddy Roosevelt was very much in favor of fair chase hunt, and his principles even inspired what we know and love as teddy bears. In 1902, Roosevelt was in Mississippi, and his hosts arranged a black bear hunt. However, the President was unable to locate any bear. One of Roosevelt's assistants cornered and tied a small black bear to a tree and requested President Roosevelt to shoot it. Roosevelt found shooting a tied bear very unsportsmanlike and refused to kill it. As the news about the bear spread, a political cartoonist read the news and drew a caricature in the Washington Post. The cartoon inspired Morris Michtom to make a stuffed toy bear, named it Teddy's Bear, and dedicated it to the big game hunting President who refused to shoot a bear.[3]

There are several methods that the hunters have used, some of them follow the fair chase principles, and some don't. Some basic techniques used are stalking, still-hunting, driving, sitting up, calling, and tracking.

Stalking is the most used when the game is timid and will run away at the slightest hint of being hunted. The hunter tries to get as near as possible and will try their best to avoid making noise. They will consider the wind direction so that their scent isn't carried away to the game. The hunter usually wears camouflage and ghillie suits to avoid detection. When the game is in the dense foliage where stalking isn't possible, then the hunters usually do stand hunting or blind hunting. The hunter waits for the prey in a concealed or elevated position and for the prey to come in range before shooting them.

Some hunters consider tracking more challenging as it requires a deeper understanding of the environment and the quarry. The tracking focuses on the footprints, signs, trails, or spoors. Spoors may as well include scats or feces, feathers, kills, drag marks,

---

[3] The Story of the Teddy Bear - Theodore Roosevelt Birthplace National Historic Site (U.S. National Park Service). (2021). Retrieved from https://www.nps.gov/thrb/learn/historyculture/storyofteddybear.htm#:~:text=Morris%20 Michtom%2C%20a%20Brooklyn%20candy,called%20it%20'Teddy's%20Bear'.

scratching posts, sounds, marking posts, and scents.

Baiting is one of the standard methods of hunting that is used around the world. If you are hunting a leopard on a safari, you need to place a smaller dead animal like an antelope high in the tree. In bear hunting areas, baits are readily available at gas stations and hunting trophy stores. The hunter usually stays undercover while a mixture of sweet substances, like molasses, is placed with rotting meat or fish.

Some hunting methods are not considered ethical or in accordance with the fair game chase. These procedures include calling, driving the herd in a particular direction, flushing, netting, posting, shining a bright light to confuse the game, and trapping using snares, pits, and deadfalls.

As hunting methods evolved, the hunting gears and weapons became too. Before scoped rifles and shotguns, humans used to use simpler tools like stone knives, spear tips, arrowheads, and knives. Humans used to pursue their game on foot, and their range was very limited, and they also carried the risk of being trampled or gored by the animals. Somewhere along the time, humans decided to use projectile hunting tools, which they used for war and fighting. Typical examples include the bow, sling, and boomerang in Australia.

In the early 1500s, single-shot muzzle loading rifles came

into use, but they were not practical for hunting. They were cumbersome and required a lot of time to steady for aim before making a shot. The loading system required a slowly burning fuse, which had a strong scent and gave out smoke before taking the shot.

While it was an improvement over the traditional bow and arrow, but it wasn't stealthy and gave away the position, and the game would run away. The rifle was improved by using the wheel-lock mechanism to fire a shot. However, it required a spanner wrench to wind up, and if the hunter lost the spanner, then the gun would become useless. Wheel lock rifles were replaced by flintlock firearms, which required a piece of flint in the weapon. While it was an improvement over the wheel lock rifles, the gap between the spark and the shot made it very difficult to hunt. Flintlock rifles were replaced by percussion ignition rifles, which reduced the time between the spark and the shot. However, the delay was long enough to warn the quarry to escape before the blast reached them.

When we started using self-contained cartridges, it was perfect for hunting on long distances. Hunters have made millions of kills using the earlier models only, and the self-contained cartridges made way for bolt-action and semi-automatic rifles. Rifles are the most accurate hunting weapons, especially with mounted telescopic sights, like the Remington Model 700. Bird hunting is usually carried by shotguns, which fire multiple projectiles in a single shot. Hunting shotguns are shoulder-fired and typically have a shorter effective range, like Winchester Model 1912 or a 12-gauge break-action shotgun. For a more minor games like squirrels, rabbits, and vermin, air guns and rifles are also used; for example, Winchester, Remington, and Walther.[4]

While automatic firing rifles were used for hunting, but nowadays, it is frowned upon by the hunting community. The automatic rifles don't give any chance for the game to make an escape and ruin the hide and meat due to multiple bullet holes. The fair chase rule also prohibits the use of automatic rifles.

Apart from weapons, dogs and falcons have been hunting partners with humans for ages. A hunting dog can be used for a variety of reasons, and different breeds are specific to other purposes. Hounds are used to locate quarry; sighthounds are known for their keen eyesight and speed, while scent hounds are slower and hunt by scent. Some examples include whippet, greyhound, redbone coonhound, and beagle. On the other hand, retrievers find and retrieve a shot animal back to the hunter, like Chesapeake Bay retriever and golden retriever. Pointer dogs, like English Cocker Spaniels, German Shorthaired Pointer, English Setter, and Poodle point, flush and sometimes hunt small game.

---

[4] Metesh, L. (2021). Hunting History: How Firearm Tech Changed the Way Americans Hunt. Retrieved from https://freerangeamerican.us/hunting-history-firearms/

Small animals like squirrels, rabbits, and birds are hunted in the Middle East using falconry. The birds used in falconry are red-tailed hawks, Harris hawk, golden eagles, sparrow hawks, peregrine falcons, and kestrels.

People from around the world participate in hunting and contribute to the economy. The money earned in hunting is usually spent on improving and breeding livestock and hunting game. The game animal's reserve requires a lot of funding, often gained by hunting expeditions.

Moreover, taking hunting up as a hobby is beneficial for you. When you are hunting consistently, not only are you putting the money that goes towards improving the ecosystem, but you can also help cull over the vermin population. Hunting is a multipurpose sport, as it requires the use of different weapons, tools, and a lot of physical strength and stamina. While hunting, you improve your survival skills by familiarizing yourself with various rifles, shotguns, ammo, scopes, knives, and binoculars. Your environmental awareness improves along with your focus, and your tracking skills are sharpened. The skills you learn while hunting can be used for your survival if needed.

Hunting can also bring you closer to nature as you acquaint yourself with wildlife, their pattern, instincts, habits, and ecosystem. You know your prey and may stalk them for weeks, which means that you are spending a lot of time in the wild. You get to know about different animals, insects, and plants, especially about dangerous insects and poisonous mushrooms, berries, and fruits. At the same time, you also learn about what things you can eat to survive if needed in the wild. You also know to apply first-aid and how to deal with emergencies, which can be used anywhere.

It would help if you were physically fit for hunting effectively, as you have to spend a long time in the woods. The long walks, lifting heavy gear, careful stalking, and even controlled breathing require physical fitness. If you are not fit, hunting might be the best motivation to get in shape. Moreover, the adrenaline rush that you gain when you successfully hunt a game is as good as any other excitement that you might get from extreme sports.

Hunting entails planning's before and after a season ends; hunters are required to prepare traps, blinds, and baits. It would be best if you also scouted the woods, trained dogs, and maneuvered through the woods, shorelines, and mountains. Besides physical workouts, hunters also require mental training, as you learn to control your breathing and nerves. You also know to hone and use your sixth sense while hunting and stalking. A hunting session can act as a natural antidepressant and lower stress and blood pressure.

As you go on hunting trips, you will make a lot of new friends. Hunters usually go out in a pack, and you can easily find a hunting group if you join a hunting lodge. You can immerse yourself in the hunting community, where the hunters stick together and look out for one another. You can make your own hunting trip if you have friends who are interested in hunting. Or, if you want to get off the grid for a while and enjoy peace and isolation from the hustle and bustle of your routine, then you can go on a solo hunting trip. You can easily forget your busy life and immerse yourself in the hunt just like your ancestors. But remember! You need to have a lot of experience before going on a solo trip; it's always better to look for an outfitter who can accompany you.

Finally, hunting is the best way to acquire chemical-free meat, as you can get your own food which is entirely natural and killed by you. When you eat your kill, you will experience a unique feeling that every hunter enjoys. It may seem paradoxical, but hunting will make you appreciate your game more. When you stalk your target for days and weeks, you realize the importance of the kill and the time you spend with it. Every kill and trophy has a personal story, and you will make your own stories when you go hunting.

Taking hunting up as a hobby is a long way to go if you are just starting. You need to learn about the basics of hunting gear and methods before you actually step into your camouflage suit. As you go into the next chapter, you will start learning about the basics, and I hope you will use that information soon.

Chapter 2
The Basics of Hunting

Hunting isn't picking up your favorite weapon of choice and shooting in the direction of the quarry. You need to strategize your trip and plan well in advance. The hunting method you choose depends on the animal being pursued, terrain, season, and your hunting tool. In this chapter, you will learn about different techniques that hunters use worldwide. You will also learn about the basics of pursuing, harvesting, and taking steps after the shooting. While there are various methods, you need to find out which way is ideal by contacting the local outfitters or authorities.

Hunting Methods

Hunting Strategies can be categorized by purpose, pursuing methods, or weapon categories. We are going to talk about different purposes hunters pursue their targets. Then we will go into pursuit methods, and finally, the choice of weapon.

Culling or Conservative Hunting

This type of hunting is usually sanctioned by the government or local authorities to conserve ecosystems or avoid damage by the animal in question. For instance, New Zealand has initiated the culling of Himalayan Tahr, as they don't have any predators except for humans.[5]

Meat or Subsistence Hunting

Meat hunting is the oldest reason that people have hunted animals. The goal is to harvest animals that the family or community can consume, and it has been a common practice in tribes and villages in many countries. However, some people hunt animals to avoid store-packed and processed meat because hunted meat is much healthier and more natural.

Sport or Trophy Hunting

The most common type of hunting is probably why you're interested in it. Sport hunting is no different than meat hunting or culling; however, hunters follow fair chase principles strictly when they are sport hunting. The hunters focus on survival skills, improving awareness and mentality, and giving a fair chance for the quarry to escape.

Hunters' Pursuing Methods

Now let's focus on different pursuing methods hunters use, including still hunting, stand hunting using calls, baits, traps, and using vehicles and dogs for hunting.

---

[5] Himalayan tahr control operations. (2022). Retrieved from https://www.doc.govt.nz/parks-and-recreation/things-to-do/hunting/what-to-hunt/tahr/tahr-control-operations/

Spot and Stalk Hunting

In New Zealand, the most common and sought-after method by hardcore hunters is spot and stalk hunting. Hunting enthusiasts use spot and stalk hunting to bag deer, Red Stagg, elk, tahr, wild boar, hogs, and feral goats. The hunter sneaks into the animal premises and tries to spot or glass (using the binoculars) the animal and take the final shot. This method requires great skill and patience, so new-time hunters often hire outfitters and guides to help them. Nonetheless, our ancestors used to do the same, and sport hunters argue that spot and stalk hunting gives a fair advantage to their prey. Spot and stalk hunting also requires walking very slowly, avoiding producing any noise, and scanning the environment for movements and other wildlife. The hunter puts themselves in danger, facing not only their quarry but other obstacles like thorns, insects, and poisonous plants. Experienced hunters will take the wind direction seriously, as their smell can warn their target, and they may escape before you even get a chance to look at them. The hunters keep themselves downwind, meaning the wind is blowing away from the direction of the animal. Let's talk about the basics of spot and stalk hunting; Tracking.

Tracking in Still Hunting

Sports hunters must be excellent trackers and understand the hunted animal and the landscape. Tracking focuses on the patterns of the animal routine and surrounding ecology. The main clue you can get to track your target is by looking for spoor. Spoor includes tracks, footprints, kills, scratching posts, sounds, trails, scat, and scents. The hunter must make predictions about the quarry's possible location using the signs and spoors and follow them. It is challenging to differentiate between different animal spoors, and the trackers' experience is vital here. Once the hunter finds a tracking pattern, it is easier to predict the quarry's location and save time by monitoring more. Apart from looking for spoors, detailed knowledge of the terrain is a must. Some landscapes, like rocky or mountainous regions, make tracking difficult. The hunter then moves to a softer ground, where there are more chances to find a footprint. In a dense area, like a forest or jungle, the hunter will look between bushes, near berries, plants, and near trees. However, in the open spaces, the hunter will most likely pay attention to the calculated position of the animal instead of wasting time looking for signs on the ground.

It is also essential that the hunter remains in stealth mode so the quarry isn't alerted to the hunter's presence. Dry leaves and twigs are carefully avoided so that there's no unnecessary sound made.

As the hunter gets close enough to shoot, they should ensure that they have a steady aim and are hidden from plain sight. Hiding in the bushes, using camouflage and a ghillie suit, and sometimes, kneeling for a long time is required. If the hunt is in long grass, the hunter may need to lay on their belly and move forward using elbows. Still hunting is the most challenging method, but the satisfaction of getting a shot is above all.

Calling

Calling is one of the basic stand hunting techniques, where the hunter uses an instrument to call or imitate animal sounds. Game calls are usually used in the mating seasons of the target quarry, and mating calls are the easiest to lure your target. Calling is made more effective by using the animal or its prey's scent to attract or even using a decoy that resembles the animal.

Some hunters make hunting calls using their hands and mouth, while others use hand instruments or electronic devices. The type of sound used to attract the animals is crucial; for instance, there is a different sound for a female deer in heat to attract a male deer. On the other hand, grunt calls or rattling antlers will attract an aggressive buck to enforce its dominance.

Other than whistles and clicks, hunters use hand calls that you put on your mouth and blow or suck the air to make the sound. Mainly hand calls are used for waterfowl, turkey, deer and other animals.

Another type called a box call is made of cedar or walnut wood. When its pieces are rubbed together, it sounds like clucks, yelps, and gobbles. A more accessible variant is a push-pull call, which has a plunger that you can easily pull or pull to imitate sounds.

We also have diaphragm calls, which can be exterior or interior. Both types contain a latex which produces different sounds by moving your mouth in various ways. These calls are usually used to attract animals.

Finally, we have electronic calls, often looked down upon by traditional hunters. The sounds are usually recorded in a studio and played by a button push.

Baiting

Baiting is very popular and influential in attracting quarries; however, you must check with the local laws before. The simplicity of this method makes it a widely used practice before rules and regulations were placed to stop the mass killing or capturing of animals. The hunter uses an artificial food source as bait. For predators, small animal is used.

Hunting Weapons

The preferred weapon choice can also categorize hunting methods. The three most common weapons used for hunts are rifles, shotguns, and bows.

Rifle Hunting

The most common form of hunting worldwide is rifle

hunting. Rifles are long-range weapons that can easily penetrate the thickest of animal skins. The rifles are highly accurate and very loud; patience is important because if you miss the shot, all other animals will be scared away. Rifle hunting is also preferred as the animal dies quickly and without much suffering. These are mainly used for animals like the Red Stagg, elk, Tahr and Chamois.

Shotgun Hunting

Where rifle is known for their long-range and efficiency, shotguns are used to increase the spread of the shot because of its close range nature. Shotguns are used to shoot at a large number of birds at, as there are a number of lead balls that spread as the range increases. While the accuracy is affected, you are most likely to injure the animal due to a high number of pellets or balls.

Muzzleloader

A muzzleloader is the most challenging hunting weapon for hunters who want to hunt on an expert level. It is an obsolete rifle where you load the pellet or bullet from the tip of the barrel, and it is fired using flint and gun powder.

Using a muzzleloader is difficult as reloading takes time, and aiming requires a lot of adjustments. But it is still great for Big game, for example for Deer its 45 Cal, Elk 50 Cal and Moose 54 Cal.

Bow Hunting

Bow hunting is a primal hunting method that predates any other weapon used nowadays. While the arrows move fast, they are nowhere as fast as the bullets, so you must get close to the target before letting one loose.

Hunters usually practice in a range before going out in the wild. A misplaced arrow can hurt the animal, causing it to get infected, succumb to infection, and die. So, hitting the right place is essential for a humane and quick death. Bows are good for all kinds of birds because of their silent attack, big game or small.

The Hunting Process

Now that you know about different hunting methods, let's see how you can use one to successfully hunt your desired quarry. Remember that a significant part of your hunt consists of preparing and researching before heading out. So, the hunting process is divided into the following simple steps:

Step One: Research before the hunt

The first step is to determine what kind of game you are after, as it will influence the method, weapon, and location of your hunt. You can choose from small games. Or, you can decide on one of the big games. If you are not experienced, it is best to leave predatory animals.

Then you need to check which weapon you are most comfortable with. If you are inexperienced with big game hunting, you wouldn't be using a bow and arrow or a high-powered gun to hunt a small game.

The best practice is to hire a guide or outfitter to help with these decisions and set up your hunting trip. You also need to check the local restrictions and laws before deciding on the hunting method. Many places prohibit traps, rifles, or certain animals from being hunted. It is always better to research before getting in trouble with the law.

Finally, you need to decide on the hunting strategy you will use. If you are hunting small animals, you can use dogs to accompany you, while migratory birds are best hunted from blinds and high seats. You can decide between blinds, stalking, tree stands, or using calls for big games.

Step Two: Prerequisites for hunting

Safety is important for you and your hunting party, so you must be trained in weapon handling and first aid procedures. Getting a hunting license is a must as you will undergo training while getting the license.

Before you pick up your rifle, you need to pack your hunting bag. It should include medication, cell phone or walkie-talkie, rain gear, fire starters, cups, flashlights, survival knife, first-aid kit, emergency food and water, and an emergency shelter if you have to spend the night out.

You must practice your tactic before you head out, which may include setting up tree stands, blinds, tracking, and stalking. Moreover, don't forget to scout the location where you intend to go hunting.

Step Three: Knowing Your Weapon

A clean shot should be your preference without damaging the game's hide and meat. Choosing an overpowered weapon will ruin your game and render it useless to eat or skin. While the types of weapons will be discussed further down the chapters, here is a summary:

a) Shotguns with twenty or twelve gauges are preferred for small game birds like quail and dove.

b) Larger gauge guns are used for turkeys, grouse, geese, pheasants, and ducks.

c) Rim rifles with hollow-point bullets and air-powered rifles can be used for rabbits and squirrels.

d) Centerfire rifles with smaller calibers are used for deer, antelope, and sheep. Similarly, bows and muzzle loading rifles can be used as well.

e) Small caliber rifles are used for wild boar, Large caliber for big game. These rifles are designed to overcome a charging animal.

You need to get familiar with the weapon by assembling and dissembling, changing the scopes, and using the iron sights. You should also know whether your gun is single-shot, pump-action, double-barreled, or semi-automatic. Each weapon is handled differently, and they have different troubleshooting techniques. You would want to be fixing your rifle while an aggressive attack charges at you. Practicing with your weapon is essential until you are confident that you can handle it in any circumstance.

Step Four: Finalizing Plans

After scouting the hunting location, you should be familiar with the terrain, animals, and the spots where you would be. You need to make a checklist to ensure you do not forget anything because you are putting your life at risk in the wilderness. The checklist should include checking up on the weather and forecast for the next few days. Your family and friends should be informed that you are leaving on a hunting trip; they will look for you in case you get in a hunting accident. Finally, you must ensure that you have all the necessary permissions from authorities and the land owners.

Step Five: The Hunt

Your vehicle should be parked at a distance from the hunting location so that you can enter the area quietly. Your eyes should observe everything everywhere; spoors can be found anywhere, and you need to be aware of the tracking skills and details. If you are blind hunting, you need to ensure that you are not attracting any attention to yourself and avoid getting your scent out in the wind.

You have the target in sight, but before taking the shot, you must ensure it is the right target. You can use binoculars or scopes to confirm, as some species are legally prohibited from hunting.

After confirming the target, take a minute before pressing the trigger. Your shot should be clean, and your quarry must not suffer by your hands. It is your duty to ensure that the animal goes down painlessly and quickly. A shot from a long distance can result in injury that will prolong the suffering, and by the time you get to the animal, it may limp away from your reach. Some other precautions must be taken before firing:

- Don't shoot if you are unsure of the background, as there could be an overkill.

- Don't shoot if the quarry is in front of a highway or populated area.

- Don't target the limbs; instead, go for the heart or the neck.

You may not make a clean shot, which is likely on a few early hunting trips. In that case, you need to track down the wounded animal and end its suffering as humanely as possible. You may need to track through challenging terrain and for a long distance. However, you might catch up quickly if you wait an hour or so before tracking the animal. Always remember that you have to follow up on every shot,

Step Six: After the Hunt

After you have shot the animal, you should start field-dressing the animal while the body is hot for the big games. The animal should be gutted quickly, and the meat must be taken out to be cooled. Make sure you are not wasting meat and leaving the carcass near a road, track, or water source. If you think you cannot carry a large animal, it is best not to shoot it. Large animals require containers as big and an SUV to carry around five to seven hundred pounds of meat. Small game animals can be bagged, but you need to ensure that you do not exceed the bag limits. Game birds must be plucked and dressed immediately, while rabbits and squirrels must be skinned and dressed before stiffening.

Remember, hunting is an age-old activity. If you follow the precautions, respect the hunted animal and their habitat, and be aware of your and others' safety, your hunting trip will be one of the best experiences of your life. These were all the basics of hunting; we will learn about hunting gear in the next chapter.

Chapter 3

Hunting Gear

Hunting is a dangerous sport, so it is best to be prepared for anything. This is why hunters require specific gear before going out to hunt for their prey. This is why I have focused on explaining all the essentials you need and more before you venture into the wild. Since you have a solid understanding of hunting basics from the previous chapter, hunting gear should not be too challenging. I am essentially letting you know how you can be safe out there and have all the gear with you. To start off, I will discuss the bare essentials you require for your hunting expeditions.

The Essentials

The essentials include your basic backpacks, boots, protective gear, clothing, and other things. While the basic gear would be the same for hunting all types of game, some of it may vary. It also depends on the environment and season. However, there are some basic items that are essential for any hunting trip: I have listed them below so you can check these off when you go shopping for your hunting trip.

Waterproof Mountaineering Boots

Your terrain may vary, so wearing waterproof mountaineering boots with good traction would be best. These boots will help keep your feet dry and stable in rugged terrain. If you have to cross any small river or swamp, your boots will remain dry.

Waterproof Hunting Jacket, Camo Pants, and Base Layers

A durable, waterproof hunting jacket will keep you warm and dry in wet or chilly weather conditions. It also doubles as protection on top of other layers you have worn. It would be best if you paired the jacket with camouflage pants with reinforced knees and a seat. These are ideal for hunting in rough terrain. The jacket is great to wear, but it needs to be on top of the appropriate base layers. Those would help you stay warm in cold weather. Wearing thermal underwear, wool socks, and a moisture-wicking shirt would be best.

Warm Hat, Gloves, and Camouflage Clothing

A warm hat and gloves are essential for keeping your head and hands warm in cold weather. Camouflage clothing helps you blend in with your surroundings and stay concealed from your prey when you are in the jungle. Wearing a warm hat and gloves is also advisable as they help keep your head and hands warm in cold weather.

Backpacks, Spotting Scopes and Binoculars

If you have ever gone on any outdoor expeditions like hiking or even mountain climbing, you would always carry a backpack. A backpack is essential for carrying gear and supplies. It is safe storage for your gear, and I would even recommend that the backpack is waterproof. You can get those from any website or physical store that sells hunting equipment, and most of those will come with a waterproof rain cover. You can pretty much store all your hunting gear, food, and water. Sizes vary, and you could choose the size depending on what you plan to carry with you on your trip.

You can find backpack on Globalsafarisworld.com. I highly recommend reading reviews for all your hunting gear so you know what brands other hunting enthusiasts prefer. Besides backpacks, binoculars are handy for scouting the area and spotting the game from a distance.

Spotting Scopes and Binoculars are essential for hunters,

allowing them to spot the game from a distance and assess the animal's size, age, and health.

Game Calls

When you are hunting, you may need to lure your prey into a position where you can easily mark them and take a shot when they become visible. This is where game calls come in. Game calls by name sound like the "calls of the wild." They can mimic the sounds of different animals, such as turkeys, elk, Red stag, fallow deer, and ducks, to attract them closer to the hunter.

Hunting Tools

The following list contains several hunting tools you should keep with you on your trip. While I have included rifles and knives in this list, you will learn more about weapons later in this chapter. Having said that, hunting tools vary depending on the type of game you are hunting and the hunting method you use. Here are some common hunting tools that hunters use:

Rifles, Shotguns, and Archery

The most common weapons used for hunting are rifles and shotguns. Choosing the right firearm for the game you are hunting is vital, ensuring that it is appropriately sighted in and maintained. Archery hunting has become increasingly popular in recent years, and archers use bows and arrows to hunt big game, such as deer and elk.

Hunting Knives

A hunting knife is an essential tool for field dressing and skinning game. Furthermore, it can also be used for a variety of other tasks, such as cutting rope, opening cans, and more.

GPS and Trail Cameras

A GPS device can be used to mark the location of a hunting spot or a downed animal. It can also be used to navigate unfamiliar terrain. Trail cameras can be used to monitor game activity in a hunting area, allowing hunters to plan their hunt more effectively.

Flashlights and Headlamps

It would be best if you carried flashlights and headlamps for use in low-light conditions or for tracking game at night.

You have to be careful when hunting because you could potentially be the hunted too. This is where emergency equipment comes in.

Emergency Equipment for Hunting Sports

When heading out on a hunting trip, preparing for emergencies is essential. Anything can possibly go wrong unintentionally or if you do not exercise caution. Therefore, you should definitely check out these vital emergency equipment items below.

First Aid Kit

A first aid kit is an essential item for any hunting trip. It should include basic medical supplies such as bandages, antiseptic wipes, pain relievers, and insect repellent.

Survival kit

A survival kit should include essential items such as matches or a lighter, a knife, a whistle, and a compass. It's also a good idea to have a map of the area and an emergency shelter, such as a space blanket.

Satellite Phone or Emergency Beacon

In case of an emergency, it's crucial to have a way to communicate with the outside world. A satellite phone or emergency beacon can be used to call for help in remote areas where cell phone reception is poor.

Water Filtration System

A water filtration system can be used to purify water from streams or other sources in case of an emergency. It can also help filter water for drinking, especially when you want to quench your thirst.

Emergency Food

Non-perishable food items such as energy bars, jerky, and dried fruit can be included in an emergency kit in case you are stranded or lost for an extended period.

Multi-Tool

A multi-tool can be useful for a variety of tasks, such as cutting rope or opening cans.

Personal Locator Beacon

A personal locator beacon (PLB) is a small, lightweight device that can be activated in an emergency to send out a distress signal that rescue teams can pick up.

Spare Batteries

It is always a good idea to bring spare batteries for any electronic devices you bring with you, such as a flashlight or GPS device.

It would be best if you always remembered that the best way to handle an emergency situation is to be prepared and to have a plan in place. Make sure you are familiar with the emergency equipment you bring and know how to use it. Additionally, always let someone know where you are going and when you plan to return.

Weapon and Accessories

Finally, we come to weapons and accessories, where you will learn about all those excellent rifles, shotguns, and other firearms that can help you do what you have set out to do in the wild! You will finally feel like a true hunter when wielding these!

When it comes to hunting weapons and accessories, there are a variety of options available, depending on the type of game you are hunting and your personal preferences. Here are some standard hunting weapons and accessories:

Firearms

Firearms are used for hunting a variety of game, including deer, elk, and birds. There are many different types of firearms, including rifles, shotguns, and handguns. I have covered each of these later on in this list.

Bow and Arrow

As stated earlier, bows are used for hunting deer, elk, and other big game. There are several types of bows, including compound bows, recurve bows, and longbows, that you can choose from. A compound bow is a popular choice for hunters. Arrows are used with bows and come in a variety of types and materials, such as carbon, aluminum, or wood. The choice of arrow depends on the type of bow used and the game being hunted.

Hunting Knives

As previously stated, hunting knives are used for skinning, gutting, and preparing game for cooking. There are many different types of hunting knives, including fixed-blade and folding knives.

Rifle

As discussed earlier, a rifle is a common hunting weapon for the big game, such as deer, elk, Tahr and Chamois. There are many different types of rifles available, including bolt-action, lever-action, and semi-automatic. You would require proper training and practice before using them the first time, and it is assumed you would have a valid license before using them.

Shotgun

A shotgun is another standard hunting weapon, particularly for birds and small game. Shotguns come in various gauges and styles, such as pump-action or over/under. Similarly, to rifles, please get the requisite training and licenses before using them.

Ammunition

It would be wise to ensure that you have the appropriate ammunition for your chosen weapon and game. You must also check local ammunition and hunting regulations to get the right and legal ammunition for your rifles and guns.

Scope

A scope can help improve accuracy when using a rifle. There are many different types of scopes available, including fixed-power and variable-power. You can aim a lot better with scopes, so having at least one kind of scope for your rifles is advisable.

Sling

A sling can help you carry your rifle more comfortably while hunting, so do purchase that with your rifle.

Range Finder

A range finder can help you accurately determine the distance between you and your target. This can help you plan your moves correctly.

Gun Case

A gun case is essential for protecting your weapon during transport and storage. It is especially helpful when moving between hunting destinations.

Hearing Protection

Wearing hearing protection, such as earplugs or earmuffs, is important when using firearms. These can get super loud, so you can literally blow your eardrums out without proper protection.

A Word of Caution

Before we conclude this chapter, I must reiterate a few

important things to remember when hunting. It would be best to always use hunting weapons safely and responsibly and check local regulations and laws regarding their use. Additionally, make sure you are familiar with your weapon and its accessories before heading out on a hunt.

As stated in the beginning, essential clothing and hunting wear depend on the type of game you're hunting, the environment you're hunting in, and the season so get the ones you require for the hunting trip you are planning. Finally, one thing to remember is to ensure that you have the appropriate licenses and permits.

Hunt responsibly, and you will have an enjoyable time out in the wild.

Chapter 4
Hunting in New Zealand

Hunting in New Zealand is considered a national pastime, and as per research, national parks allow hunting on their premises. You would also be surprised to know that New Zealand does not have any native game animals except for two species of bats. This has been the case since human settlement, so the animals now residing in the national parks were also settlers, just like their human counterparts. Interestingly enough, one of those bat species is now extinct. There were also two Otariidae species.

Thanks to European immigrants, land mammals made their first entry onto New Zealand soil. There were two kinds of animals. One was specifically for game hunting, and the rest was for farming and other purposes. Interestingly, the United States gave New Zealand elk/wapiti as gifts from President Theodore Roosevelt. It is also believed that Americans had inhabited whitetail deer on the island south of New Zealand

Acclimatization societies, starting from the 1860s, were active for a good 60 years once the animals were introduced, of which most were kept for sport and food. The Recreational Hunting Areas, or RHAs, were established to provide support for recreational hunting on conservation land. These RHAs are supervised by the Department of Conservation to endorse conservation land recreational hunting.

The Name of the Game

There are two ways to hunt in New Zealand: guided and non-guided. Both are available for non-resident hunters having a firearms license and permit issued by the Department of Conservation. The varied terrain and availability of large game species have made New Zealand an exciting hunting destination for hunter-tourists worldwide.

As you can see, it is fun to hunt in New Zealand because there are not many restrictions. A permit will do you good, and even better if you have experience hunting. It is a great place to relax outside of hunting because there is so much to see, from wildlife to urban nightlife. New Zealand is one of the lands down under, but it should be on your go-to list as a hunter-tourist. Deer is wildly popular, and a variety of those will be available to hunt. There is more on deer hunting in later chapters, but for now, you must know that New Zealand comes across as more hunter-friendly than other places.

There can be issues as the terrain varies and adds to the challenge of the hunt. Now, what good is a hunt if the game does not give you a proper challenge? Whether it is a chamois, Tahr, deer, or wild pig, each game animal offers its challenges, so you will have plenty to test yourself with there.

Ticket to Hunt

A Department of Conservation (DOC) hunting permit is required to hunt in all the areas open to licensed hunters for hunting. There are different permits depending on where and what game animal you choose to hunt. The areas you can gain permits are as follows:

- The open-area hunting permit

- Restricted area hunting permit

- Small game hunting permit

- Game bird hunting permit

The DOC website has tons of information available on permits and how to access them. I have touched on it here so you have a fair idea, and you can choose to check out the website for further details.

Open-Area Hunting Permit

The open-area hunting permit is free of cost and is a necessary requirement for hunting in open areas. The permit allows you to hunt ground-based and non-commercial hunting of chamois, wallabies, goats, deer, and pigs. These areas are operational under standard hunting permit conditions. Some open areas may require special conditions. For example, the permit may be invalid during busy times when that area is blocked or balloted. In those cases, a separate dog permit would possibly be required.

Te Urewera hunting permits require registration from an independent body, so do check out the DOC website on how to obtain permits for that. Otherwise, you can always apply online or on-call for the standard permits.

Restricted Area Hunting Permits

As the name states, these permits are issued for restricted areas. If you want to noncommercial hunt ground-based deer, chamois, tahr, deer, goats, and pigs, you would require this permit. Furthermore, these can be issued for open area non-standard hunting. This would apply to muzzleloaders, for example. These areas come with special conditions, such as limited-period hunting.

Small Game Hunting Permits

It would be best if you had a small game hunting permit from DOC for the recreational hunting of small game animals on public conservation land. Small game includes Canada geese*, feralgeese, hares, and rabbits (which are unprotected game animals). Not all regions have small game hunting areas available, so call the local DOC office first.

Game Bird Permits

A separate permission is required for hunting game birds on public conservation land. This is in addition to the game bird hunting license to be obtained from Fish & Game NZ. These are also used for particular periods and areas like restricted area permits. You can have these issued via the local DOC office that supervises the site. Note that not every region includes game bird hunting areas, so it is best to check with the local DOC office first. If you want to hunt Canada or feral geese, you would require a small game hunting permit because they are considered small game animals/ birds.

Playing Possum- Possum Permits

You would require a special possum permit to hunt them on public conversation land. Furthermore, some of these possum locations are supervised via a block system. This means one permit holder can utilize one block. This is done on a balloted or first-come-first-serve basis, and you would need to check this with the local DOC office. The same office issues the permits depending on the hunting area. Furthermore, possums are not available in all regions, so you would need to inquire from the local office first before planning your hunt.

Other Concerns

You would require permits to use poison like cyanide and also to lay traps. The assistants at the local offices will assist you, so you would need to submit additional documentation when applying.

License to Hunt

When in New Zealand, you have a license to hunt game animals with the correct permits. Thankfully, these permits are not so hard to acquire, but please hunt responsibly when out in public conservation lands. You can visit the DOC website to get forms and other information.

(https://www.doc.govt.nz/parks-and-recreation/things-to-do/hunting/permits-and-licences/hunting-permit/).

The thrill of the hunt is when there is less red tape to worry about, and that is what makes New Zealand an excellent hunting destination. You would still need to do the necessary homework before you travel down under and get familiar with the area. It would also be best, and I must highly recommend that you take the assistance of local guides to point you to the best hunting spots. Otherwise, the internet is always your best friend. You have the license to hunt, so when you go there, make the best use of that license!

Chapter 5
Top Go-To Places for Hunting

It has been stated in previous chapters that European settlers were responsible for game animals, and the only native mammal species were bats. Those animals made the country their home, as there were no natural predators. Population control is accomplished via controlled and safe hunting. Most game targets include deer, which further include fallow, sika, and red. Others include possums, goats, pigs, and tahr. Some hunting expedition companies will offer upland game bird and first-rate waterfowl hunting.

Tools of the Trade

It works best to use a commercial hunting guide. What happens is that guided big game hunting costs a lot of money, so it is best to go for cheaper local options. These are more geared toward the conservation hunting side than making money. It also works best to join local hunting clubs. Hunters n a work vacation or extended break settle in a New Zealand town or city and search for local hunting clubs on the internet. You will encounter experienced hunters you can learn from.

You can also partake in WWOOFing. Working tourists will find accommodation at a farm. Look for those WWOOFing profiles that are specific to hunting, and let the hosts know you want to learn. This will help you get ready for the hunting trips.

Location Guide

Manawatu-Whanganui

The North Island is home to remote hunting locations in the forested Manawatu-Whanganui region. You will find wild pigs, goats, and fallow dear for hunting with companies like Remote Adventures close to Waitotara. You will find goats, deer, and pigs when you explore the Whanganui National Park. These are situated in Blue Duck Station backpacker-style farm.

Wellington

There are three forest parks located in the Wairarapa District of Wellington, which are known as:

- Tararua

- Rimutaka

- Aorangi

You can also hunt deer in some exciting coastal properties with agencies like Wildside Walks.

The South Island

Nelson/Tasman

Nelson Lakes National Park is home to goats, pigs, fallow, tahr, and chamois. This is your chance to hunt small game ducks, including black swans, geese, pukeko, pigeons, ducks, quail, rabbits, hares, and possums. Strike Adventures is recommended to contact for your hunting trips there.

Canterbury

The Canterbury region is home to some hunting trip farms, including Kaiwarua Station and Caberfeidh Farms. These are also known as Hunter Hills. You can also check out Te Kahui Kaupeka, Hakatere Conservation Park, and Conservation Park to hunt rams, goats, tahr, and red deer.

Otago and Southland

There is plenty of game to hunt in the Hawea Conservation Park. You can look toward local hunting guides to scout for tahr, chamois, and red deer. If you dig deeper into Fiordland National Park from Te Anau on a jet boat, you can enjoy guided fishing and hunting.

The Duck Factory

Hunters have been intrigued by New Zealand's "Duck Factory." Waterfowl hunting became prevalent in the Waikato/Hauraki area of New Zealand. It eventually became known as the Duck Factory. The residents of the Auckland/Waikato region are blessed with the most amazing waterfowl hunting the country offers. I would say it is perhaps the best in the lands Down Under. These residents can access it by traveling for an hour on the road from Auckland City. The primary wetland areas under the ownership of the Crown and Fish & Game are public access areas through boat ramps, walkways, and roads. Maps are available online, but it is best to explore and seek information from white baiters, hunters, eelers, sports shop employees, landowners, and other groups; you can increase your knowledge of your specific area tenfold.

Fish and Game and Crown Land Hunting

You can acquire a General Authority, which reportedly costs nothing to license holders for hunting on Fish & Game Land. It stretches for 1700ha and is under the ownership of the Auckland/Waikato Region, bought from anglers' and hunter's funds. You can gain a similar permit to hunt on Crown Land, which is under the management of the Department of Conservation

Forest hunting permits

If you are a fan of quail hunting, you could head to the several Rayonier Forests in the Auckland/Waikato region. You can gain abundant quail and pheasant hunting opportunities. You can get the permits from the Hamilton office of Auckland Waikato Fish & Game Council. Each permit is suitable for all four forests, public liability insurance, and colored maps when you hunt in the Rayonier forests.

The Auckland/Waikato Duck Factory

Hunters should get the excellent 48-page booklet by Auckland/Waikato which is perhaps the only guide you need for game bird hunting in that area. It comes with proper text and maps, and you can simply get it free of cost by sending an application in a large, stamped, self-addressed envelope.

Guidelines for Maimai Construction

There is pressure on modern hunters from others who are not fluent in waterfowl hunting traditions. Those hunters are required to build and manage their maimais, which gives waterfowl hunting a positive image. You could gain a pamphlet for permanent maimais guidelines published by Auckland/Waikato Fish & Game, Land Information NZ, Department of Conservation, and Environment Waikato. It is recommended to read for rookies and experts. You could also get this free by sending in a stamped, self-addressed envelope.

Hunting in New Zealand is an experience because the non-native mammals residing there make for excellent game animals and birds. We covered a wide range of hunting areas, and these are universally considered the best hunting spots in the country. You can read more about these through other online resources, and this chapter is an excellent place to start your research. You have understood how to get permits and save costs on guided hunting tours.

As always, please be careful when you are hunting. All of the information presented in this chapter is sourced from different online resources, as the idea was to get the information in one place so you can get started easily. The Duck Factory is a recommended hunting trip should you venture to New Zealand. The wide variety of land mammals offers different challenges too. Have fun but hunt responsibly!

Chapter 6
Big Game Hunting

As stated in the earlier chapters, game hunting has been an active sport for the longest time. It was launched by some of the renowned European settlers in New Zealand. The New Zealand government, too, endorses legalized animal hunting in most of the prime mountainous localities within New Zealand. This book is a guiding light for hunters or swashbucklers to take the lead in big-game hunting. To help the readers swoop into extracting the most out of the "hunting extravaganza," it is equally essential to learn the details of the hunting games available in the heart of the hunting world; New Zealand.

New Zealand is the hunters' hub, where passion meets the

hunter's eye. New Zealand provides hunters the joy of life, of heavenly breathtaking and picturesque landscapes, superb trophies to having one of a lifetime hunting experience. Targeting hunting animals with heavy ammunition is a mind-boggling experience that the New Zealanders offer. Notably, the government makes suitable regulations and policies to cater to hunting expeditions for tourists and seasonal hunters. As depicted by hunters, the spine-tingling roar of the rutting red stag undoubtedly draws much attention to New Zealand, irrespective of other recreational opportunities the land provides.

Game Hunting in New Zealand is considered a well-supported outdoor sport for adventurers and hunters. It is for those who love to take the lead in hunting animals that breed around stunning sceneries and mountainous areas. It includes a wide range of animals, precisely the deer species, such as red, sambar, sika, fallow, whitetail, wapiti, and rusa. These species are primarily widespread across New Zealand or found in small populations in specific areas. Other species include wallabies, pigs, and goats. For hunting guides, occasional hunters, or otherwise, the Roar season is the most exciting for hunters to hunt male stags during their mating season. But, mind you, with hunting comes preparation, practice, and passion.

New Zealand has undoubtedly helped in conserving the natural ecological environment through hunting. By the time people began migrating to New Zealand, many introduced animal species that were a pest to nature's atmosphere, the farming sector, and the licensed forestation departments. Hunting animals, by date, have no natural predators known to humans. Hence, for New Zealanders, hunting has become one of the leading outdoor sports that grabs much attention from the outside world. Not only does it aid with reviving the hunting industry, but it has also helped the country's tourism sector to gain "the good grip."

As mentioned, hunting requires patience and perseverance. If hunting independently, the expedition should be planned well before arrival. A person who plans hunting should be well-versed in having a licensed firearm before applying for a hunter's license. One of the best courses of action for visitors who wish to hunt is accompanying a qualified New Zealand hunter's license holder. Travelers interested in hunting must do the right research before leading toward an exploration hunting procedure. First, the excursion should be planned so that the hunters can gain experience to the fullest. If going with a group or otherwise, the planner should consider the skills and fitness available to the group members. Hunting requires risk-taking. A local hunt or an adventure will all have its risks. One needs to consider what to expect first carefully. The leader of the group should duly gauge the sort of vehicle that will be required and whether the group will be camping on the hunting side. To hunt, one must check the weather forecast in case of unalarmed torrential rain at mountainous locations. Keeping a GPS phone or a compass would help the team members track their location. Usage of binoculars and the affiliated tools should be maintained along, that too, right before planning a hunt or an expedition. Some famous hunting locations in New Zealand are far from residential areas, so it is crucial for tour guides to plan the hunt before the sun goes down. To know the tropical sense of the hunting location, the hunter must also know the features of the land with respect to the river, steep hills, bluffs, and ridgelines.

To familiarize the readers with the ample big games available in New Zealand, I will mention some renowned hunting species that are the hunters' most favorite. Some of them are as follows:

Red Stag – The Pinnacle of New Zealand Big Game Animals

For several reasons, the red stag is ultimately the main focus of many New Zealand hunters. As per some discussions with hunters, they call the Red Stag the "Pinnacle of New Zealand big game animals."

Around 1851, the European settlers launched their beloved big game, the red deer. The original New Zealand red deer stags (male) and hinds (female) are descendants of the Scottish Red Deer and were later mix-bred with Hungarian bloodlines to increase their body and antler size. Over the years, New Zealand estates continually improved the genetics of their herds. Many of these massive stags can be found in large estate properties and free-range lands.

New Zealand is the best location to hunt stags with big bodies and oversized antlers. New Zealand hunters regularly take 400 SCI stags on the hunting estates, while some exceed 600 SCI. Undoubtedly, red stags are much more expensive hunting expeditions than the trophy elk hunt in the States. Some seasonal hunters have SCI record books that reveal the prolific population of the red stag in New Zealand. Many free-range hunts have considerably smaller stags than can be found on estate hunts, but red stag hunting is always a breathtaking experience.

Besides the hunting animals available in New Zealand, Red Stag hunting is essential and intensely sought after. The hunters, too, take keen pride in hunting the red stag for recreational purposes and as part of their achievement in hunting history.

Red stag is also known as the magnificent trophies hunted in many parts of the world.

The European red deer is one of the world's only hunting animals on every continent except Antarctica. It is native to Europe and Asia and some other widespread species on both continents. Some lesser-known deer, the Barbary red deer, are native to North Africa, Algeria, Morocco, and Tunisia.

So, if you want to hunt red stag, almost the entire world is your playground. Before hunting a red stag, one must remember some crucial questions before execution. Is it essential to hunt a native range? How about a free range? Want a big stag or a good hunt for a nice stag? What about timing? Personally speaking, hunters hate reality, but the budget and timing of the hunting are the central part of the discussion.

Red stags are categorized into categories affiliated with good quality and under reasonable costs, of which the native range is of much talk among the hunters.

Most red stag hunting is free range throughout Europe and western Asia. The red deer are farmed, ranched, and bred for so long that no region is entirely free of high fences.

Outside of Europe, Argentina, and New Zealand are the primary destinations. They have free-range red deer in vast areas that involve active deer breeding and game ranching industries. It makes the hunting a mix. As per research, there are some excellent red deer in Texas and elsewhere in North America.

New Zealand is famous for producing the world's largest red stags. In the 19th Century, European immigrants introduced red deer in the rugged hills above the farmed valleys. Finding an ideal environment with the absence of predators is crucial.

Deer farmers brought in superior genetics and are producing magnificent stags, but New Zealand's biggest stags are the big ones that are typically lesser in quantity. Research shows New Zealand has excellent unfenced stags in the hills above the deer farms. However, in the backcountry, "genuine" free-range New Zealand stags still have modest antlers.

A red stag private land hunting area encompasses 80,000 acres of low fence premier red stag country. Hunts are conducted daily from base camp and takes place on foot.

A red stag of approximately SCI 280 – SCI 320 is considered free-range trophy quality. It is uncommon to see genuine free-range stags exceeding SCI 315. New Zealand harvests a sustainable number each season due to comprehensive hunting management. Red stags are increasingly active throughout the Autumn months.

There is something truly remarkable about hunting a genuine wild New Zealand red stag. Nothing can quite excite the hunter than the hair-raising sound of the red stags fighting for a harem of hinds. Hunting a roaring red stag is one of the most unforgettable and exhilarating experiences.

Premium red stags are commercially raised and genetically enhanced for New Zealand's deer farming industry. Red stags are purposely bred for the finest first-class red stag trophies in the world.

Red stag is found on both the North and South Islands. With very little game management, stags on government land typically grow much smaller antlers due to feed, genetics, and taking out the larger dominant breeding males.

As discussed, the Red Stag and its affiliated hunting style, the chapter will further discuss the types of deer available for hunting in New Zealand.

Tahr

The Mighty Tahr is a prized <u>mountain trophy</u> located in the Southern Alps of New Zealand. The Tahr originated from Nepal and Tibet and was introduced in 1904.

One of the most prized in New Zealand, the Himalayan bulls have remarkable climbing power. This makes the Tahr the best hunt, even for the most seasoned and physically fit hunters. A <u>Tahr</u> can weigh up to 300 lbs and have remarkable mobility and climbing ability for their size.

For tourists and visitors who cannot climb mountains, the government of New Zealand has given hunters access to helicopters to reach the mountaintop for the desired Tahr hunting experience.

Chamois

Originally from the mountains of <u>Europe</u>, Chamois live in New Zealand's steep mountain slopes on the South Island. It was first introduced in New Zealand in 1907 as a gift from the Austrian Emperor, <u>Franz Joseph I</u>.

<u>Chamois are agile antelope</u> that enjoy rugged, rocky terrain and alpine grasses with high altitudes. <u>These animals are challenging to hunt</u> due to their habitat and sharp eyesight.

In the summer, the Chamois have rich brown fur that develops into gray and sometimes black during the winter. The winter coat of Chamois's fur makes for a fantastic rug and other dresses or harsh weather. Chamois hunting is, indeed, a memorable mountain hunting experience. Due to the challenging terrain, <u>very similar to Tahr hunting</u>, the government arranges helicopter lifts to and from remote mountaintops.

Fallow Deer

Aside from their unique, palmated antlers, fallow deer are famous for their vivid coats. They come in three color phases: chocolate brown, spotted menil, and white.

<u>Fallow</u> Deer in New Zealand are of Danish descent and were introduced in 1860 by European settlers. A smaller species of deer

in New Zealand have genotypes with differing color phases, i.e., standard, melanistic, menil, and white. They are often found in bushes closer to pasture/farmland, as they prefer grassgrazing. Significant herds are located in the North and South Islandsof New Zealand.

Fallow deer are found both in the North and South Islands of New Zealand, with the most concentrated population being in the Mackenzie district, central South Island. Fallow deer can be aggressive and may cause injury or even death to each other. They can be hunted both wide free range or on estates by spot and stalk, calling, or sitting over a rutting pad and waiting. The male deer's have their rutting pad that they guard while they wait for the female to come in during the rut and get served. Fallow deer are the only species other than moose with heavy palmate antlers.

Elk/Wapiti

These animals are indeed a monstrous class of hunting in New Zealand. The <u>South Island Elks or Wapiti</u> originate from the bloodlines of the mighty Rocky Mountain Elk.

The elk rut usually coincides with the red Stag from March to April, presenting an extensive hunting opportunity that can be hunted all year round.

Sika Deer

New Zealand Sika deer are found only in the central North Island of New Zealand. Their rut also coincides with the red stag from late May to the end of April. These small spotted deer are aggressive and have a high-pitched squeal during the rut. Sika deer can be hunted on private and government land, with the main hunting season from March and extending until July.

Rusa Deer

Due to small population numbers, rusa deer hunting in New Zealand is limited to the North Island and mainly on private estate land. As an Asian deer species, the rusa typically ruts in July and is much larger than the sika deer because the stags are also very aggressive toward each other. The antler's length can reach upto 35+inches, and they are renowned for the quality of their meat.

Sambar Deer

The second largest deer species in the world, sambar deer are the most challenging animals to hunt in the South Pacific due to their shy nature. These 500+ pound animals live in thick native vegetation that requires patience. Three small herds are wild and free range in the North Island, mainly on private lands, with some herds on private estates. These herds have been caught by helicopter and relocated to the estate. Heavy antler formation has the reputation of having a robust flavor taste in the meat.

Remember, hunting is for the risk-takers and the go-getters. So it is essential to guide your hunting team to duly familiarize itself with the do's and don'ts of hunting and be prepared to visualize a one-of-a-lifetime hunting experience of the red stag or other hunting animals if you plan to visit New Zealand any time sooner.

Chapter 7

Mountaineers Who Hunt

As a seasonal hunter, I have come to an understanding that hunting requires in-depth research. Without that, you can't make up to even a percentage of living the hunting life. As discussed in my earlier chapters, hunting is about grit and passion. The experiences and shortcomings that the hunters face vary largely. Most of my hunter friends and my followers have shared their own experiences with me, and I'd say that hunting has got to be a challenge not everyone can take. Some fail, some fall, some rise, and some go beyond, but very few succeed. By the time you hop on this chapter, you'd feel like you missed out on the good perks of life. I'd suggest my readers to deeply go beyond the book if they need to reach a hypothesis of "the hunting life." I might sound boring to some, but this book holds some of my personal experiences and hunting adventures that I've had the pleasure to experience. It is the best example of man vs. beast, to begin with, and I am proud to compile all of these in one nice book.

To begin with, I'd let my hunter readers learn about the difficulties and challenges many hunters face in the mountains. The pros and cons of hunting in the mountains will be deeply discussed so the explorers may be well versed in efficiently planning the excursion before settling for a voyage. Further discussed are some challenges that most hunters face, if not all. So, without further ado, let us begin!

Rightly Facing Your Fear

Some hunters say, "To conquer fears, you must embrace it, not go beyond it." If you're hunting solo or otherwise, it is essential to understand that embracing fear is easier said than done. Going solo into the mountains, one needs to wear their strength on their sleeves but not go overboard. You must respect fear. It is also essential that the hunter must not go beyond their mental or physical threshold. Hunters never admit to being afraid or nervous. Hunting is a sport that is more of a hurdle for the weak hearts. Fear, risk-taking, and preventive measures top the list when planning a mountain hunt. It's the minds game to adequately cater to an evident fear or a hurdle that comes the way.

Fitness

When hunting, you must know your limitations and how your body can survive. It is not advisable to push your body beyond its limits. Otherwise, you might find it hard to survive in the wild. Most mountaineers emphasize keeping the body fit as it helps with an easy climb. The same goes for hunting. Hunters are very much open to injuries and risks when exhausted. Hunters out there risk their lives to hunt, which at most times, is not an easy catch. Most hunters are physically fit and lean who easily survive the topography, extreme Weather, and survival conditions.

Safety Measures

Like taking a risk, it is sufficiently important to address safety measures. When hunting in the mountains, one must be efficiently prepared with all the safety tools. Carrying a cellular phone with a GPS is crucial if one finds himself lost in the wild. The hunter must also have a portable charging system in the safety toolbox to avoid running out of signals and batteries. Hunters should never go unprepared with weapons. Staying hydrated by drinking a lot of water is essential so bring a camelback not energy drinks or shots that will dehydrate you. Most times, hunters struggle to move across destinations and the perfect hunting spots where the target hunt is easily achievable.

Weather

One of the most essential things on the hunting checklist is to closely monitor the weather forecast. Weather in mountainous regions and high localities is moist and damp. Hence, the chances of an apparent downpour are high. The hunters should plan the hunt when the weather forecast doesn't notify of any monsoon or torrential rains so the target is efficiently met. Most hunters plan hunts for as long as months apart; executing a successful hunt takes intense courage and team unity. The steep hills of the mountains, too, become slippery, so the hunters have a hard time gripping onto their safest positions for rest or planning a night camp otherwise.

Efficient Food Supplies

Hunting on the mountain makes one pack for food supplies rich in nourishment and power-packed with energy. Keeping along some smoked salmon sandwiches and a leafy green salad makes the hunter survive the cold nights on the camp. You need to be hydrated so drink a lot of water to help hunters stay wide awake to hunt the animal because hunting requires; being guarded at your feet at all times.

These tips helped me execute my hunt smoothly. And kid you not, I had the most amazing time hunting my favorite animal, the Himalayan Tahr. I remember my first professional hunt was planned for months on end, and I was adamant to pull it off with all my might. Needless to say, I made the most out of the hunting memories that I will cherish forever.

I've hunted many animals in the past, but the hunt of the Himalayan Tahr is my most prominent achievement. If any of my readers have little interest in the big game, they would be astounded to learn about the Himalayan Tahr and the perfect way to hunt it.

The Himalayan tahr is a large goat-like mammal with horns that reaches a maximum length of 18 inches. The males weigh around 160 pounds, and the females weigh half the males. The Tahr has a naturally dense, velvety woolly coat that keeps it warm during cold nights on the mountain. The Tahr's coat lightens in color and becomes thinner during the warmer seasons. They have developed an ability to live on smooth and rough surfaces. Even on the mountainous terrains, the Himalayan Tahr uses even-toed hooves with rubbery cores. The Tahr's head is proportionally small, with large eyes and small pointed ears. The horns are triangular and curved abruptly backward. This prevents severe injury in head-butting battles during mating season.

The Himalayan Tahr is native to parts of the Himalayas. However, it has also been found in some hilly areas in Argentina and the United States areas. With the help of the thick, velvety coats,

Himalayan Tahr remains comfortable in cool climates with rocky and rough topographical locations. They stay active in the morning and late afternoons and take short breaks in the middle of the day to rest between rocks and vegetation. It feeds on vegetation and spends most of its active time grazing on grass and bushes. Their features entail tiny legs that help them to reach the trees and shrubs in mountainous areas. The Himalayan Tahr has a multi-chambered stomach like the cow, allowing it to digest nutrients and hard-to-eat plants.

Himalayan Tahr females have multiple mates, making the males compete for their spot. Most Himalayan Tahr males usually have a light-colored coat, a large mane, and horns. Females complete a seven-month span to deliver their offspring. The babies naturally have the strength to move around shortly after birth, and they mostly depend on their mother's feed for about six months but stay close to for up to 2 years. In the wild, the Tahr will live about ten years and up to 20 years in captivity. The closest living relatives to the Himalayan Tahr are sheep and goats.

Himalayan Tahr usually lives in mixed herds of about 15 members. They survive well with invasive species that relocate to different countries. The Tahr's digestive system allows them to digest various food. The Himalayan Tahr is one of the three species of Tahr. Other Tahrs are the Arabian Tahr of Oman and the Nilgiri Tahr of southern India. The Himalayan Tahr is the wild goat's relative and is specially adapted to live on the Himalayas' rugged mountain slopes and woodlands.

During the breeding season in October through January, the male Himalayan Tahr ruffs up to intimidate its opponents. It tries to impress the females with their appearance before mating. When challenged by another male, they lock horns and throw each other off their balance. The Nilgiri and Arabian Tahrs are rare due to hunting and are listed as vulnerable and endangered by the World Conservation Union (IUCN). The Himalayan Tahr is considered vulnerable and is a trophy prize for hunters worldwide.

The Himalayan Tahr is regarded as the King of the Mountain. It lives in the highest mountain peaks of New Zealand's Southern Alps. Tahr hunting is expensive for their horns and their thick lion-like mane. A bull tahr can weigh as much as 300 lbs. It has a dark body, and straw-colored hair thickens and lengthens from late April. The Tahrs utilize difficult terrain to their advantage and are remarkably agile. It is one of the most difficult trophies to obtain. A Tahr hunt largely tests the skills of even the most seasoned world-class hunter. The Tahr rut extends from May through early August but is fun and thrilling at any time of the year.

Speaking about the Himalayan Tahr brings in the discussion of Chamois or the Shammy leather that grabs the attention of many hunters and tourists. Further explored are some features of Shammy leather and how it helps revoke fashion in the leather industry. Although made from the skins of a goat or antelope species, it is native to European mountains. Chamois cloths are made from sheepskin leather that is tanned with marine or fish oils. The definition of Chamois differs from country to country. Also known as the "Shammy," the natural leather is durable, absorbent, and exceptionally soft. It can quickly dry surfaces without scratching them in the process. It is mostly preferred in producing drying towels. The Chamois helps naturally pull dirt and grit away from the surfaces. Unlike other drying towels, a chamois will effectively release the trapped dirt without making the towel abrasive over time. Unlike synthetic drying products, authentic leather chamois are natural and reoccurring. It is mostly the byproduct of sheep ranching used for food production.

In conclusion, I would like to discuss my hunting expeditions wherever I went. That are the only memories that I want to cherish forever. So back when I visited New Zealand, I was much anticipated for my journey. I flew into the North Island and flew to Christchurch. My friends and I drove from Christchurch down to South Omaha. A couple hours of drive later, we reached the Treadwell, located to the South. We hunted the red stag and the Arapawa Ram while I hunted Feral goats and the Tahr. New Zealand is more like a mountain range on Island. So I flew into the Island where the terrain was just plain mountains.

When I hunted, I had to hike toward a high elevation to get to a good location for the hunt. Hunting on the mountain or the hills require more physical strength than hunting on land. When I was there, it was the wintertime in New Zealand. I saw snow on the ground and even on mountain peaks. While in some places, the sky was clear with little fog and rain. The typical mountain weather is very unpredictable. It was sometimes quite sunny and hot one day and would be cold the next day. To get the good hunt or make the achievement, I remember I had to camp on the hill and stay vigilant to get my target right. I remember traveling in the truck to the mountain landscape, where we parked my vehicle far away from the hill and hiked to the top. Unlike the red stag, the hunt for shammy and Tahr was much harder since they lived on much higher peaks. Outfitters usually work with privately-owned helicopter companies to take the game out of the woods and drop off clients in remote areas with not-so-easy access for a better hunting experience, especially chamois and Tahr hunts, since they are pretty demanding physically.

I've always loved hunting in New Zealand, but mostly for the red stag. When I went there, the hunt turned into a Tahr hunt. I hunted Tahr. That's like the mountain goat of New Zealand. Tahr is challenging, and the right hunt is judged by the inches of the horns. I have achieved the good trophy by hunting the 12-inch horned Tahr.

For me, the Tahr hunt was the highlight. It was a hard-earned hunt of which only I know the struggles that words won't do even justice to. I hiked the mountain up and down. I was tired, but I never wanted to give up. It was a big deal for me when I finally shot my red stag. I shot it in 2 hours. I really wanted to hunt the Tahr since they are cool animals.

Chapter 8
Small Hunting Games and Bird Hunting

As you have read in previous chapters, New Zealand is known for its diverse wildlife and stunning natural landscapes, making it an ideal destination for small game and bird hunting. The country has a unique and varied ecosystem that supports a wide range of hunt able species, including Wallaby, hare, rabbit, possum, and various hunt able bird species.

The climate and topography of New Zealand also make it an ideal place for small game and bird hunting. The country's mild temperatures and great hunting conditions all year round provide countless opportunities for hunters. Furthermore, New Zealand's varied terrain provides a variety of hunting settings, ranging from rugged mountains to open fields, forests, and wetlands, making for an exciting and challenging hunting experience.

Furthermore, strict hunting regulations and conservation efforts in New Zealand ensure that hunting activities are sustainable and do not harm the environment. The country has created hunting seasons, quotas, and laws for each species to ensure that populations stay stable and healthy. This responsible hunting technique has helped to preserve New Zealand's natural balance and its distinctive fauna for future generations.

Explaining Small Game and Bird Hunting

Small game and bird hunting are popular outdoor activities in New Zealand due to its abundant and diverse wildlife. Small game animals like Wallaby, hare, rabbit, and possum, as well as varied species of huntable birds, provide ample opportunities for hunters to engage in an exciting and challenging hunting experience.

For instance, Wallabies are pretty widespread across New Zealand and are sought for their meat, which is considered a delicacy. Hare hunting is another popular activity, particularly in the Central Otago region, which has a significant hare population. Another popular attraction is rabbit hunting. The country's large open expanses provide plenty of possibilities to hunt these small creatures. Possums are also heavily targeted in New Zealand since they are considered a pest and can cause major damage to the ecosystem.

In terms of bird hunting, New Zealand has a wide variety of species available, including pheasants, quails, partridges, and waterfowl, among others. These birds are also frequently hunted for their meat, which is also regarded as delectable, as well as their colorful feathers, which are utilized in crafts and decorating.

New Zealand's hunting regulations ensure that hunting activities are done in a sustainable and environmentally friendly manner. Before engaging in hunting activities, hunters must get permission, and hunting seasons, quotas, and laws for each species are tightly enforced to ensure that wildlife populations stay stable and healthy.

Small game and bird hunting in New Zealand provide avid hunters with a memorable and exciting outdoor adventure. For hunters in search of a new and exciting hunting experience, this country has it all: a wide variety of species, a wide variety of landscapes, and a strong commitment to conservation.

Significance of Small Game and Bird Hunting

Culture and History

Small game and bird hunting have played a significant role in New Zealand's culture and history. The hunting of small game and birds is deeply ingrained in the country's heritage, and it continues to be an essential activity for many New Zealanders.

An Ideal Destination

New Zealand's diverse landscape and rich biodiversity make it an ideal destination for hunting small game and birds. From the dense forests of the South Island to the rolling hills of the North Island, the country offers a wide range of hunting experiences for enthusiasts. Some of the most popular small game and bird species hunted in New Zealand include rabbits, hares, possums, ducks, geese, pheasants, and quail.

A Way of Life

For many New Zealanders, small game and bird hunting is a way of life. It is a way to connect with nature, harvest food sustainably, and maintain traditional hunting practices that have been passed down from generation to generation. Hunting is also an important aspect of New Zealand's rural economy, providing jobs and income for many people in rural communities.

Conservation of New Zealand's Wildlife

Small game and bird hunting also play a critical role in the conservation of New Zealand's wildlife. The hunting of some species, such as possums and rabbits, helps to control their populations and reduce the damage they cause to the country's ecosystems. Hunting also contributes to the monitoring and management of bird populations, as hunters provide valuable data on the number and health of different bird species.

Regulated by the Department of Conservation

Hunting in New Zealand is regulated by the Department of Conservation (DOC), which sets quotas and manages hunting seasons to ensure the sustainable use of wildlife resources. The DOC also works closely with hunters and hunting organizations to promote responsible hunting practices and to educate hunters about the importance of conservation.

In conclusion, small game and bird hunting are an integral part of New Zealand's culture and history, providing recreation, food, and income for many New Zealanders. Hunting also plays a critical role in the conservation and management of the country's wildlife resources, ensuring that future generations can continue to enjoy the unique hunting experiences that New Zealand has to offer.

Wallaby Hunting in New Zealand

Wallabies are an invasive species in New Zealand. They cause significant damage to the country's natural environment, especially in the South Island.

Hunting wallabies is an important activity that helps control their populations and reduce their negative impact. Wallaby hunting is also a popular recreational activity in New Zealand, attracting hunters from all over the world.

Species of Wallaby Found in New Zealand

There are three species of wallabies found in New Zealand: The Bennett's Wallaby, the Dama Wallaby, and the Parma Wallaby.

The most commonly found species is the Bennett's Wallaby, which lives on the South Island, while the Dama wallaby lives on the North Island, and the Parma wallaby lives in the Wellington region.

Hunting Season and Regulations

Wallaby hunting in New Zealand is permitted throughout the year, except during the breeding season, which is from November to February.

Hunters need to have a valid hunting permit and follow the regulations set by the Department of Conservation. These regulations include restrictions on weapons types and ammunition that can be used and the number of wallabies that can be hunted per day.

Wallaby Habitat and Behavior

Wallabies in New Zealand are found in a variety of habitats, including grasslands, shrub lands, and forests. They are most active during dawn and dusk and are known to be quite elusive. Wallabies are herbivores and feed on a variety of plants, including grasses, herbs, and shrubs.

Wallaby Hunting Techniques

Wallaby hunting in New Zealand can be done using a variety of techniques, including stalking, shooting from a hide, and using dogs. Stalking involves quietly moving through the Wallaby's habitat and waiting for an opportunity to take a shot.

Shooting from a hide involves setting up a concealed location near a wallaby's feeding or watering spot and waiting for the Wallaby to appear. Using dogs involves training dogs to track and flush out wallabies, making them easier to spot and shoot.

Wallaby Meat and Recipes

Wallaby meat is considered a delicacy in New Zealand and is known for its lean, tender texture and mild flavor. Wallaby meat can be cooked in a variety of ways, including roasting, grilling, and stewing. Some popular wallaby recipes include wallaby burgers, wallaby stir-fry, and wallaby curry.

Hare Hunting

Another popular hunting in New Zealand is Hare hunting. It requires skill and patience, and there are many techniques that hunters use to catch these elusive animals.

Techniques

The most common techniques used by hunters in New Zealand for Hare hunting are:

- **Stalking**

Stalking is one of the most common techniques used by hare hunters. This involves slowly and quietly moving through the woods or fields in search of hares. Hunters often pause frequently to listen for any movement or sounds that might indicate the presence of a hare.

- **Beagling**

  Beagling is a type of hunting that involves using a pack of beagles to chase hares. Hunters release the dogs in an area where hares are known to frequent, and the beagles will chase the hares until they are caught.

- **Netting**

  Netting is a technique that is used to catch hares in open areas where they are more visible. Hunters set up a net in an area where hares are known to be commonly found and then chase them toward the net. Once the hare runs into the net, the hunter easily catches it.

- **Shooting**

  Shooting is another popular technique used by hare hunters. Hunters use a shotgun or other type of firearm to shoot the hare when it comes into view. This technique requires a lot of skill and accuracy, and it's important to be aware of the local hunting laws and regulations.

- **Hotspots**

  The Department of Conservation (DOC) offers few opportunities for rabbit and hare hunting. Contact the DOC office closest to the hunting area for information on opportunities and permission requirements, among other things.

The majority of suitable habitat is located on private property, requiring the landowner's permission to access.

Hares can be found across New Zealand's North and South Islands, occupying suitable habitats ranging from sea level to 2000 m. Parts of South Westland, Fiordland, and an 80-kilometer radius north of Auckland are devoid of hares.

Any type of grassland or open area, coastal sand dunes, pastures, rush-covered places, and clearings in scrub or forest are also favorites for hare hunting. Hare hunting requires skill, patience, and a good understanding of the techniques and hotspots that can be used to catch these elusive animals.

By using the right techniques and hunting in the right areas, hunters can increase their chances of success and enjoy this popular sport. However, it's important always to be aware of local hunting laws and regulations to ensure that hunting is done safely and legally.

Possum Hunting

Possum hunting is a popular outdoor sport in New Zealand, where possums are a major threat to the environment due to their impact on native flora and animals. Possums were brought to New Zealand for fur trading in the nineteenth century. However, they have since become a nuisance species and are now considered a severe danger to the country's natural ecosystem. As a result, possum hunting has become an essential component of New Zealand's conservation efforts.

Thermal Imaging Technology

Possum hunting is typically done at night in New Zealand with dogs, traps, or thermal imaging technology. The most frequent approach is dog hunting, which involves using specially trained dogs to track, chase, and tree possums. Possums are swift and nimble climbers, so this demands a great level of expertise and experience.

Trap Hunting

Trap hunting entails placing baited traps in places where possums are known to be active.

Thermal Imaging Equipment

Thermal imaging equipment is used to detect possum heat signatures, which can then be used to track and hunt them more successfully.

Possum hunting is not only a method of population control, but it also allows hunters to interact with nature and the great outdoors in New Zealand.

13 Huntable Birds Species in New Zealand

Game birds are 13 bird species that can be hunted periodically in New Zealand. They are classified as upland game and waterfowl.

The pheasant family includes all upland game that lives on dry land. They are as follows:

- Ring-necked pheasants

- California, brown and bobwhite quails

- Grey, red-legged, and chukar partridges

Wetland game birds include:

- Four duck species: mallards, grey ducks, Australasian shovelers, and paradise shelducks

- Black swans

- Pūkeko

Grey partridges and bobwhite quails are still on the game list, but they are no longer found in the wild in New Zealand.

All of these species are classified as game under the Wildlife Act of 1953, and they are administered by regional fish and game committees. Hunters who obtain a game bird license and obey the restrictions can lawfully hunt these species during specific seasons (typically autumn and winter).

Native and Introduced Birds

The grey duck, paradise shelduck, Australasian shoveler, black swan, and Pūkekoare were indigenous to New Zealand, whereas the other eight species were introduced.

Other Introduced Hunted Bird Species

Some birds that are not listed as game birds in the Wildlife Act are also hunted. The Cape Barren geese, greylag goose, wild turkey, and peafowl are among them. The Canada goose was classified as a game bird until 2011, when it was delisted. It is no longer protected and can be hunted at any time of year and with any method.

Hunting Times

Upland game is typically hunted in the middle of a bright, sunny winter day. Traditional duck hunting, on the other hand, is done early in the morning or late in the evening.

Hunting with Dogs

To be lawfully shot, birds must be flying and within 30-50 meters of the hunter with a shotgun. Upland game hunting requires a well-trained and professionally handled gun dog, as these birds rarely take to flight unless flushed by a dog. Dogs should not move any further than the distance that a hunter can fire at a flushed bird. The hunter must shoot the bird within seconds of it shooting up from ground cover in a whirl of wings.

Dogs are also used to get marsh animals out of hiding and to get them out of water.

Different hunters prefer different dog breeds, which are frequently pointers, setters, or retrievers. Many hunters are members of gun-dog groups and gun clubs, and they keep their interest in dog training year-round, despite the fact that the hunting season is only a few months long in the winter.

Pheasants and Quail

Upland game hunters must be keen and hardworking, as pheasants and quail are scarce in many areas. Partridges were brought to New Zealand, although their population is still quite small. Hunting quail requires a lot of labor from the dog but little movement from the hunter other than monitoring for rapid flushing of a bird. When a covey is discovered in a gully, the hunter must either wait for the dog to flush them or sit tight for hours.

Pheasant hunting, on the other hand, may require the dogs to go considerable distances before finding their strong-smelling quarry. Only cocks are killed to keep pheasant numbers up, so hunters must use split-second judgment to target the proper birds when they are in flight.

Quail and pheasants are typically hunted in groups, with

each hunter having an equal chance of firing a shot. If they are successful, the downed bird must be recovered by the dog.

Ducks and Other Wetland Birds

Wetland game birds, including ducks of various species, are shot from shooting areas on farms as well as publicly owned canals and marshes where hunting is authorized. Hunters usually lie near the water and use fake decoys and sounds to entice ducks and geese within shooting range.

Cuisine

Most game bird hunters consume their kills or give them to friends and family. Cleaning and plucking or skinning birds for the meal is required. Wild foods have grown in popularity since the 1990s, and recipes are widely available. Most towns have restaurants that will cook game birds donated by hunters, which is a welcome change for chefs, particularly those trained in Europe, as there have previously been few opportunities to cook game in New Zealand.

Regulations

Game and Fish New Zealand has a legal obligation to manage game-bird hunting. Each fish and game council within its territory has the authority to initiate seasons for hunting specific species, set daily bag limits, and restrict the types of shots, firearms, and shooting tactics.

Hunters are only permitted to use shotguns and must shoot birds in flight. They must purchase game-bird hunting licenses, with the proceeds going to Fish and Game New Zealand to administer hunting. Unlike other nations, the government does not provide any money.

Regional councils are elected by license holders to develop policies and budgets for species management. Fish and game councils keep track of game bird populations, harvest levels, and hunter satisfaction. They make every effort to guarantee that the crop is sustainable.

Hunting is a highly regulated activity in New Zealand, and there are specific laws and regulations that govern hunting practices. Before embarking on a hunting trip, it's crucial to familiarize oneself with the hunting regulations in New Zealand and obtain any necessary permits and licenses. Conservation of wildlife is a high priority in New Zealand, and hunters are expected to hunt ethically and sustainably.

Tips and Tricks for Small Game and Bird Hunting

Since small game and bird hunting are popular activities in New Zealand, there are many tips and tricks that can help hunters have a successful hunt.

Essential Equipment

For hunting, one must have some of the most frequently used equipment:

- **Firearm**

A shotgun is a popular choice for bird hunting, while a .22 caliber rifle is suitable for small game hunting. It's important to have a good-quality scope and to practice shooting before going on a hunting trip.

- **Clothing**

Wear comfortable and durable clothing that blends in with the natural surroundings. Camouflage or earth-toned clothing is recommended to avoid startling games.

- **Other Equipment**

Carry a hunting knife, a backpack, and plenty of water. A hunting dog can also be useful in locating games and retrieving them after they are shot.

Hunting Strategies

Use the following hunting strategies for a great hunting experience.

- **Spot and Stalk**

Spotting and stalking game is common strategy used by

hunters. Look for games in open areas and move slowly and quietly toward them.

- **Driving**

Driving involves using a group of hunters and dogs to drive a game toward a designated shooter. This technique is more effective in areas with dense cover or in larger groups.

- **Calling**

Calling involves using a bird call or animal distress call to lure the game out of hiding. This technique is particularly effective in areas with low visibility, such as dense brush or forested areas.

Safety Measures

One of the most important aspects of hunting is to always have safety precautions in place.

- **Identify Your Target**

Always make sure to properly identify your target before shooting. Many game species in New Zealand are protected, and it's important to know the difference between legal and illegal species.

- **Know Your Surroundings**

When hunting, always be aware of your surroundings at all times, and avoid shooting toward houses, roads, or other people. Always carry a first aid kit and know how to use it.

Respect the Environment

Respect the natural environment by leaving no trace and following all hunting regulations. Always obtain permission from landowners before hunting on their property.

Small game and bird hunting in New Zealand can be a challenging and rewarding experience. By following these tips and tricks and taking necessary safety measures, hunters can increase their chances of success and enjoy this popular activity while respecting the environment and local laws.

Overview of Hunting Regulations in New Zealand

New Zealand has strict hunting restrictions in place to protect the country's unique wildlife and ecosystem while also allowing hunters to enjoy their sport. These rules include everything from hunting seasons and bag limits to licensing and safety. Hunting on public grounds is permitted, but hunters must acquire permission from landowners before hunting on private property. There may also be restrictions on the sorts of weapons and ammunition that can be used in certain regions.

Hunters must be licensed and adhere to safety restrictions, such as wearing blazing orange apparel during specific hunting seasons and refraining from ingesting alcohol while hunting. There are further rules governing game transportation and processing, including mandated tagging and reporting. These laws are managed and enforced by the New Zealand Department of Conservation, and infractions can result in penalties, incarceration, or the loss of hunting licenses.

Restrictions and Limits for Small Game and Bird Hunting

Small game and bird hunting in New Zealand is governed by strict rules that govern the types of species that can be pursued, hunting methods, and bag limitations. Hunting of non-native game birds such as pheasants, quail, and partridges, for example, is permitted during specified seasons, with bag restrictions varying depending on the species and locality. Some native birds, such as the endangered kiwi, are strictly prohibited from being hunted.

There are also restrictions on hunting methods, such as the use of traps, snares, or poison, which are prohibited while hunting small game. Hunters must use proper rifles and ammunition and adhere to safety precautions. Violations of these rules can result in huge fines or imprisonment.

Furthermore, before hunting on private property, hunters must obtain permission from landowners, and hunting on some public lands may be restricted or require a permit.

Consequences of Violating Hunting Regulations

In New Zealand, violating hunting restrictions can result in harsh penalties ranging from fines and jail to the revocation of hunting licenses and permits. The degree of the penalty is determined by the nature and seriousness of the infraction. For example, hunting without a license can result in a $100,000 punishment and up to five years in prison, while poaching or killing threatened species can result in a $300,000 fine and up to five years in prison.

In addition to legal consequences, breaching hunting restrictions can have serious environmental consequences. Overhunting or hunting for threatened species can have a negative impact on local ecosystems and wildlife populations.

The Department of Conservation in New Zealand is incharge of enforcing hunting restrictions and may take legal action against violators. To safeguard the safety of themselves and others,conserve the environment, and maintain hunting opportunities for future generations, hunters must be aware of and respect all hunting regulations.

To summarize, Small Hunting Games and Bird Hunting in New Zealand is a fun and exciting activity, but it comes with some limitations. When enjoyed in boundaries, it can be one of the most adventurous activities to do in New Zealand.

In conclusion, small hunting games and bird hunting are exciting activities to participate in while in New Zealand, but certain restrictions must be observed. As long as they are enjoyed within legal boundaries and with the necessary precautions, these activities can provide an unforgettable adventure for those who partake in them.

Chapter 9
After the Hunt

Hunting is the stillness of a chilly morning; it is the suspense of waiting, the adrenaline rush of seeing a game, the ease of camaraderie, and the familiarity of a unique animal. However, the significance of hunting far outweighs these scenarios.

Hunting benefits nature and the environment in a variety of ways. Hunting, more than any other outdoor activity, provides an understanding and appreciation for wildlife and the habitats inwhich it thrives. Hunting allows you to explore wild places and testyour mettle against every kind of game animal.

Furthermore, in an era when much of our food is processed or modified, the hunting lifestyle provides delicious, nutritious protein for a meal.

The Importance of Hunting

Hunting is a sophisticated and varied activity that people have engaged in for thousands of years. People hunt for a number of purposes nowadays, including subsistence, recreation, and cultural or traditional reasons.

Hunting for a Living

Hunting is a source of food for many people. Hunting was

historically the primary method by which humans obtained meat, and it continues to be an important source of protein for many communities around the world. Subsistence hunting is often done on a small scale and is strictly regulated to ensure the sustainability of wildlife species.

Hunting for Recreation

Hunting has evolved into a popular sport and recreational activity in addition to providing sustenance—many people like the challenge and excitement of pursuing game animals and the sensation of being outdoors. Sport hunting can also be used to bond with family and friends and get away from everyday life's stresses.

Traditional and Cultural Hunting

Hunting has cultural or traditional significance in some communities. It is an integral part of many Indigenous nations' spiritual and cultural practices. It is also frequently viewed as a way to connect with nature and honor the hunted animals.

Management and Conservation

In New Zealand, hunting is a controlled activity, with laws and regulations in place to manage and maintain animal populations. Hunters are frequently obliged to get licenses and adhere to strict laws regarding hunting seasons, bag limits, and the usage of specified hunting techniques or equipment. These rules are intended to keep animal populations healthy and sustainable for future generations.

While people hunt for a variety of reasons, hunting is a deeply ingrained part of human history and culture. Hunting, whether for subsistence, sport, or cultural purposes, allows people to interact with the natural world and experience the thrill of the hunt. At the same time, it is critical that hunters obey all restrictions and standards to guarantee the sustainability of animal populations.

The next step after hunting involves field dressing the animal, preserving the meat, and preparing it for consumption or storage. When you finish hunting in New Zealand, you have completed the difficult task of tracking and stalking your prey, lining up the perfect shot, and taking it down. However, your work is not done. Your next step after hunting is field dressing.

Field Dressing

If your major goal in hunting is to harvest good meat that will last for a long time, you need to be well-trained in field dressing. The significance of this critical procedure cannot be overstated, and it must be carried out correctly to avoid dangers to your health and the longevity of the meat.

Field dressing removes a game animal's intestines and internal organs to chill the meat as rapidly as feasible. This is an important procedure that must take place as soon as the animal is taken to prevent the meat from deteriorating.

The basic intent of field dressing is to keep your meat clean and bacteria-free. Bacteria begin to multiply very immediately; thus, prompt dressing is critical. After the initial dressing, the meat should be kept in a refrigerator at temperatures below 40 degrees Fahrenheit.

Proper field dressing and keeping the meat cool not only prevents bacteria but also increases its durability. Meat from your hunt can last for more than a year if properly stored.

Learning to Field Dress

As you can expect, the procedure for field dressing varies slightly depending on the animal's size. Proper field dressing of game animals after hunting in New Zealand is essential to preserve the quality of the meat and reduce the risk of contamination. Here are some general steps to follow when field-dressing game animals in New Zealand:

1. Begin by creating a shallow incision.

It would be best to start by creating a shallow incision from the base of the sternum to the pelvis along the midline of the belly. This initial cut is made to expose the internal organs by opening up the bodily cavity. The incision should be shallow enough to avoid harming the flesh and cutting into any organs. This cut requires the use of a keen hunting knife.

2. Gently remove apart the skin and abdominal muscles.

After making the initial incision, gently pull the skin and abdominal muscles apart to expose the internal organs. This makes organ removal easier and lowers the chance of harming the meat.

3. Remove the internal organs with care.

Remove the internal organs with care, including the heart, lungs, liver, and intestines, being careful not to puncture any organs and contaminate the meat. The stomach and intestines should be removed whole without being punctured or sliced.

Internal organs can be carefully removed once they have been exposed. It is critical not to puncture any organs during the removal process, as this can lead to meat contamination. To avoid leakage, the stomach and intestines should be removed intact, without being punctured or cut.

4. Carefully remove the bladder.

Remove and discard the bladder, taking care not to spill any urine on the meat. If urine comes into contact with meat, it can impart an unpleasant taste and odor.

5. Hang the animal.

Hang the animal with the head up or position it on a slope with the head down to allow the blood to flow from the body. This helps to retain the meat's quality and reduces the chance of spoiling.

The blood can be drained from the body by hanging the animal with the head up or laying it on a slope with the head at the bottom. This helps to retain the meat's quality and reduces the chance of spoiling. To keep the meat from deteriorating, hang the animal in a cool, shady area or place it in a cooler.

6. Remove any remaining blood or debris from the bodily cavity.

After removing the internal organs, the body cavity should be rinsed with clean, cold water to remove any remaining blood or debris. This reduces the possibility of contamination and ensures the meat is clean and safe to ingest.

7. Cool the animal for several hours by hanging it in a cool.

Allowing the animal to cool for several hours ensures that the meat is thoroughly cooled and safe to consume. The meat can be kept at a safe temperature by hanging the animal in a cool, shaded area or keeping it in a cooler.

8. Chop it into smaller pieces and bundle it for travel or storage.

Once the animal has cooled, it can be cut up and packed for transport or storage. To prevent spoiling, use clean, sharp knives to cut the meat and keep it refrigerated during transport or storage.

It's important to note that specific techniques may vary depending on the type of animal being field dressed and the individual preferences of the hunter. It's always a good idea to consult with experienced hunters or professional guides for guidance on proper field dressing techniques and safety precautions.

Field Dressing in New Zealand

Hunters in New Zealand often utilize one of two procedures for field dressing an animal: gut removal or the gutless approach.

Gut Removal

This process entails making a cut down the animal's belly and removing internal organs such as the liver, kidneys, and intestines. This is the most common and conventional method of field dressing an animal. It is a simple and efficient strategy that is reasonably simple to master. The main advantage of this approach is that it effectively removes the organs that can quickly deteriorate the meat. This process, however, is untidy, and there is a risk of contaminating the meat with intestinal contents.

The method involves making a shallow cut around the animal's anus, followed by another cut through the skin down the middle of the belly, all the way up to the rib cage. Cut the muscle and connective tissue carefully to expose the organs, then pull them out of the body cavity. Remove all organs before cleaning the inside of the animal with a hose or a stream of water.

The Gutless Method

The gutless procedure involves extracting the animal's flesh without entering the bodily cavity. This approach is becoming more popular among hunters because it is less messy and faster than gut removal. However, it necessitates more skill and practice than the gut removal procedure.

It is done by making an incision behind the animal's shoulder blade and then cutting down the animal's spine. Cut through the spine with a saw or knife to separate the meat from the bones. Remove the meat from the legs and shoulders before moving to the loins and back strap. While performing the gutless procedure, avoiding cutting through the stomach or intestines is critical, as this can contaminate the meat and cause spoilage.

Things to Avoid

Avoid a couple of crucial blunders while field-dressing your game since they can undo all of your hard work and leave you with inedible meat.

First, it is critical not to cut into the intestines, bladder, or stomach organs. These are all contaminated with fluids such as urine and stomach acids, as well as the contents of the animal's waste and most recent meal, all of which can easily contaminate the meat. Therefore, be careful or have an experienced person help you in this endeavor.

To avoid catching oneself with your knife, cutting with a steady and careful hand is vital. Sharp knives are desirable, but they are also dangerous, especially when working in restricted places. If you're not careful, a wound might develop into an infection, so work swiftly but carefully when field dressing your hunt.

Meat Cooling and Preservation

After field dressing the animal, the next crucial step is to cool the meat as quickly as possible. This is critical because if the meat is not cooled quickly, it will rot, and bacteria will proliferate, rendering it inedible. As a result, adequate temperature regulation is critical for keeping meat quality.

The Importance of Temperature Management

Temperature management is critical for sustaining meat quality. Meat storage temperatures should be kept between zero and four degrees Celsius. Any temperature above this range is likely to promote bacterial growth and deterioration. Keeping the meat at the proper temperature is critical until it's cooked or frozen.

Cooling the Meat in the Field

It is very critical to cool the meat immediately after field dressing to minimize bacterial growth. One method is to use ice or a cool water source. If you are hunting in a remote place without access to ice, you can cool the meat by hanging it in a shady area with a game bag. If the weather is warm, a fan can be used to help cool the meat.

Packaging and Transporting Meat

Keeping the meat refrigerated when packaging and transporting it is vital to prevent bacterial growth. To keep the meat cool, use ice packs or dry ice. The meat should be securely packed to prevent air from circulating and spoiling it. When transporting the meat, ensure that it is securely fastened and does not move, as this can cause damage to the meat.

Preparing Meat for Long-Term Storage

It is imperative to properly preserve meat if you intend to store it for an extended period of time. One approach is to freeze the meat. To avoid freezer burn, wrap the meat tightly in plastic wrap or aluminum foil. You can also vacuum-seal the meat to keep air out of it. If you intend to keep the meat for an extended period, consider curing or smoking it to extend its shelf life.

To summarize, appropriate meat cooling and preservation are crucial to preserving meat quality. To prevent bacterial growth and deterioration, preserving the meat at the proper temperature, packing it correctly, and safely transporting it is critical. You can ensure that the meat you hunt in New Zealand is of the greatest quality and safe to ingest by following these instructions.

Animal-Specific Cutting and Packing Techniques

Depending on the type of animal harvested, cutting and packing procedures differ. Here are some hunting tips for New Zealand's most commonly hunted animals:

Deer Meat

Deer meat is often sliced and packed into primal cuts, which are big animal pieces that can be subsequently separated into smaller portions. The most typical primal cuts are the hindquarters, front shoulders, and back straps. The meat should be kept as clean as possible during processing and chilled as soon as possible.

Wild Boar

Wild boar meat is rougher and gamier than deer meat, necessitating a different processing method. The meat should be hung for a few days to develop taste and kept cool throughout this period. When the meat is done, it can be cut into primal cuts such as hams, shoulders, and loins.

Game Bird

Game birds, such as pheasants and quail, require a different processing strategy than larger animals. The first step is to clean the bird and remove the feathers. After cleaning, the bird can be chopped into smaller pieces, including the breast, wings, and legs.

Other Species

The cutting and packaging techniques for other animals, such as rabbits or possums, will differ. The general idea is to keep the meat as clean as possible while processing it and to divide it into manageable chunks for travel and storage.

It is critical to remember that all meat should be correctly labeled and dated during the cutting and packaging process and stored and transported at the appropriate temperature. Hunters may guarantee that their hard-earned game is adequately maintained and ready to enjoy by using proper cutting and packing techniques.

Hide Removal and Preservation

Hide removal is a crucial stage in the preservation of meat because it allows the flesh to cool faster and minimizes the danger of rotting. Hide is the skin of an animal, and it is removed from the animal's body after it has been field dressed. Hide removal allows the meat to cool faster and reduces the risk of spoilage.

The first step is to cut around the animal's legs and then down the belly to the chest. The skin should next be detached from the body with a skinning knife. It is important to avoid cutting through the hide or nicking the meat.

Prepare Hide for Tanning or Mounting

After removing the hide, it can be prepared for tanning or mounting. The hide should be properly cleansed and fleshed to remove any leftover flesh, fat, or tissue before tanning. To help preserve the hide, soak it in a tanning solution.

If the hide is to be mounted, extra care should be given during the preparation procedure to avoid harming it. The hide should be spread out and dried on a fleshing board. It can be cleaned and preserved once dry using a variety of ways, including salting and drying or chemical preservation.

Tips for Good Hide Preservation

Proper handling and storage of the hide is essential for success. The hide should be kept cool and dry until it can be treated, preferably in a freezer or cooler. It is also critical not to use too much salt or other chemicals during the preservation procedure, as this can harm the hide. Finally, if you are confused about how to treat and preserve your animal skin properly, seek professional advice.

Each process has advantages and disadvantages, and selecting the appropriate method for the type of meat and planned usage is critical.

Taking the Trophy Home

After a successful hunt, many hunters choose to take home a trophy to commemorate their experience. Whether it's a mountable animal head or a beautiful hide, proper care and transport are essential to ensure that the trophy stays in good condition.

Choosing the Right Taxidermist

A taxidermist is a professional who prepares, stuffs, and mounts animal skins for display or preservation. When it comes to conserving your trophy, a professional taxidermist can make all the difference. Take the time to investigate and select a professional taxidermist who is familiar with the species you've hunted. Examine their previous work and check customer evaluations to ensure you make the appropriate decision.

Preparing the Trophy for Transport

Once you've decided on a taxidermist, it's time to prepare your trophy for transport. This usually entails skinning the animal, cleaning the hide or skull, and carefully packing it for transit. If you're unclear on how to prepare your trophy properly, seek advice from your taxidermist or a hunting guide.

Bringing the Trophy Home

Transporting the trophy home can be a tricky business,

especially if you're traveling considerable miles. The trophy should be properly packed and protected to avoid damage during shipping. This could include employing specialized packaging or even engaging a professional shipping firm. Again, working with a taxidermist or a hunting guide can help guarantee that your prize arrives in pristine condition.

Ultimately, proper field dressing, meat preservation, and trophy handling are critical steps New Zealand hunters must take after a successful hunt. It not only keeps the meat fresh and safe for consumption, but it also keeps the memory of the hunt alive for years to come.

Understanding animal-specific cutting and packing skills, as well as proper hide removal and preservation techniques, can significantly impact the whole hunting experience.

By following the principles outlined in this chapter, hunters can ensure that the animal's flesh and hide are preserved while also generating lasting memories of their hunting trips.

Part 2: Fishing

Chapter 10

Fishing as a Hobby

In part one, we discussed in-depth hunting in New Zealand. We took a look back in time and reminisced about the historical significance of the trade and how this has evolved over the years. We also discussed how the indigenous people used hunting in the bygone times and what practices, tools, and weapons were used. We discussed and described how hunting is used today in New Zealand for recreation and population control of various animals.

Furthermore, the hunting part included chapters on the most popular animals hunted and typical time frames, routines, or procedures that hunters must follow. It captivated readers with details of the perilous hunting setting that is a vivid feature of New Zealand's hunting sport and discussed the preferred hotspots that offer the best and most adventurous hunting experience, making New Zealand a sure shot entry on every hunting enthusiast's bucket list.

In this Fishing section, we delve into the captivating world of fishing. We begin by delving into the history of fishing in New Zealand, tracing its origins, and examining its cultural and traditional significance.

The section will review the various fishing methods and techniques commonly used in New Zealand. In addition, we will provide a researched description of the most common fish that can be hooked and reeled in and identify the go-to spots that provide the most exhilarating fishing experience for anyone who seeks it.

By the end of this section, you will have a deeper appreciation for the rich historical context of fishing in New Zealand, acquired knowledge about various fishing techniques, and developed an understanding of the physical, mental, economic, and environmental benefits of this cherished pastime.

Through this exploration, we hope to inspire readers to

engage in fishing while fostering a sense of responsibility towards the environment and promoting sustainable practices for preserving New Zealand's natural resources.

Historical Significance of Fishing

The fishing history of New Zealand is intertwined with its unique geographical features, diverse marine and freshwater ecosystems, and the cultural practices of its indigenous Maori people. Here is an overview of the fishing history in New Zealand:

Maori Fishing Traditions

Fishing has been an integral part of Maori culture for centuries. The Maori people deeply understood the coastal and freshwater environments, developing sustainable fishing practices to ensure the preservation of fish stocks. They employed techniques like nets, lines, weirs, and traps made from natural materials like flax. Fishing was crucial to their subsistence, economy, and cultural practices.

Early European Influence

With the arrival of European settlers in the early 19th century, commercial fishing practices began to emerge. European fishermen, primarily from Britain, recognized the abundance of fish in New Zealand's waters. They introduced new technologies and methods, such as larger vessels, trawling nets, and longlines, which increased fishing efficiency and developed a commercial fishing industry.

Rise of Commercial Fishing

By the late 19th century, commercial fishing had become a significant economic activity in New Zealand. Fishermen exploited the country's rich marine resources, establishing coastal fishing communities and exporting fish to international markets. The industry flourished with the expansion of refrigeration technology, enabling longer fishing trips and the export of fresh fish.

Development of Regulations and Conservation

As the commercial fishing industry grew, concerns about overfishing and depletion of fish stocks arose. To address these issues, the New Zealand government implemented regulations and conservation measures. Fishing licenses, size limits, seasonal restrictions, and quotas were introduced to ensure sustainable fishing practices and protect the long-term health of fish populations.

Recreational Fishing

Recreational fishing has always been popular in New Zealand due to its abundant fishing opportunities. As early as the late 19th century, recreational fishing clubs were established, promoting the sport and fostering conservation efforts. Today, recreational fishing remains a cherished activity for both locals and tourists, with many people enjoying fishing from the coast, rivers, and lakes.

Modern Fishing Industry

The modern fishing industry in New Zealand is highly regulated and technologically advanced. Commercial fishingvessels utilize sophisticated equipment like sonar, GPS, and advanced fishing gear to target specific species and minimize bycatch. The industry focuses on sustainable practices, including quota management systems, fishery assessments, and marine protected areas to safeguard fish stocks and protect the marine ecosystem.

Maori Fisheries Settlement

In the 1980s and 1990s, the Treaty of Waitangi settlements recognized the fishing rights of Maori as part of their cultural and historical connections to the sea. This led to the establishment of Maori fisheries entities, such as iwi (tribal) fishing companies and trusts, enabling Maori communities to actively participate in the fishing industry and manage their own fisheries resources.

Today, fishing is an essential aspect of New Zealand's identity, culture, economy, and recreational pursuits. The nation's commitment to sustainable fishing practices and conservation efforts ensures the long-term viability of its marine and freshwater resources for future generations.

Importance of fishing in Maori culture and Traditions

Fishing is deeply significant in Maori culture and traditions, vital to their history, spirituality, economy, and sustenance. Here are some key aspects highlighting the importance of fishing in Maori culture:

Connection to Ancestors and Legends

Fishing is often associated with ancestral figures and legends in Maori culture. The story of Maui, a renowned mythical hero, features prominently in Maori folklore. According to legend, Maui fished up the North Island of New Zealand using a magical fishhook. This tale symbolizes the relationship between the land and sea and the integral connection between the Maori people and their environment.

Kaitiakitanga (Guardianship) of the Sea

Maori strongly believe in kaitiakitanga, which refers to the responsibility and stewardship of the environment. This concept encompasses the sustainable management and protection of natural resources, including the sea and marine life. Fishing serves as a practical expression of kaitiakitanga, as Maori engage in practices that ensure the preservation of fish stocks and the ecological balance of the marine ecosystem.

Cultural Practices and Customs

Fishing has been integral to Maori cultural practices and customs for generations. It has been passed down through oral traditions, where knowledge of fishing techniques, fishing spots, and fish behavior is shared among whanau (family) and hapu (sub-tribes). Fishing expeditions were often communal activities, fostering social cohesion and strengthening kinship ties within Maori communities.

Food and Subsistence

Historically, fishing played a vital role in the subsistence and food security of the Maori people. The coastal and freshwater resources provided an abundant and reliable source of nourishment. Fish was a staple food in the traditional Maori diet, along with other seafood such as shellfish and kaimoana (seafood delicacies). The ability to catch fish ensured the survival and well-being of Maori communities.

Ceremonies and Rituals

Fishing rituals and ceremonies hold significant cultural and spiritual importance in Maori traditions. Before embarking on a fishing expedition, Maori would perform karakia (prayers) to seek blessings and protection from their ancestral guardians. These rituals acknowledged the spiritual connection between humans and the natural world, reinforcing the cultural values and beliefs associated with fishing.

Economic Activities

Fishing has also played a role in the economic activities of Maori communities. Traditional fishing practices provided a means of trade and exchange, allowing Maori to acquire goods and resources from neighboring tribes. With the establishment of commercial fishing in New Zealand, Maori have actively participated in the fishing industry, managing their own fisheries resources through iwi (tribal) fishing companies and trusts.

Cultural Revival and Identity

In recent years, there has been a resurgence in Maori cultural practices, including fishing, as part of a broader cultural revival movement. Maori communities have been actively involved in protecting and restoring their customary fishing areas, advocating for sustainable fishing practices that align with their cultural values. Fishing serves as a means of cultural expression, strengthening the sense of identity and connection to their ancestral roots.

Overall, fishing holds immense importance in Maori culture and traditions. It embodies their heritage's spiritual, social, economic, and culinary aspects, reflecting their deep connection to the sea and the principles of kaitiakitanga. Through fishing, Maori continue to uphold their cultural values, preserve their ancestral knowledge, and maintain their unique relationship with the marine environment.

Fishing Methods

Fishing methods are techniques and practices used to catch fish, varying depending on the type of water, target species, and desired outcomes. Understanding different fishing methods is crucial for anglers and fishing enthusiasts to effectively and responsibly pursue their favorite pastimes.

Two of the fishing methods used in New Zealand are:

- Sea fishing methods

- Freshwater fishing methods

Sea Fishing Methods

Sea fishing methods refer to the various techniques and practices used to catch fish in marine or saltwater environments. Anglers and fishermen employ these methods to target specific species, adapt to different fishing conditions, and maximize their chances of success.

Sea fishing methods encompass a wide range of approaches, including but not limited to trolling, surfcasting, longlining, jigging, bottom fishing, drift fishing, and hand lining. Each method has unique characteristics, equipment requirements, techniques, and target species.

By employing these methods, anglers can explore different depths, habitats, and locations within the vast expanse of the ocean to pursue their desired catches. Sea fishing methods play a crucial role in both recreational and commercial fishing, allowing individuals to engage with the marine environment and contribute to the sustainable utilization of its resources.

Following are the sea fishing methods that are commonly used in New Zealand:

- **Trolling**

Trolling is a popular sea fishing method that involves trailing a fishing line behind a moving boat. The boat moves slowly, allowing the bait or lures to mimic the movement of live prey. This method is effective for targeting predatory fish that swim at various depths.

- **Equipment:**

Trolling requires a sturdy boat equipped with rod holders, fishing rods, reels with line counters, and a selection of lures or bait. Downriggers or planer boards may also be used to control the depth at which the bait or lure is presented.

- **Techniques:**

Anglers adjust the trolling speed, depth, and the type of lure or bait to attract fish. The boat's speed, direction, and patterns are varied to entice strikes from species like salmon, trout, kingfish, and marlin.

- **Target Species:**

Trolling is commonly used for catching pelagic fish such as tuna, mahi-mahi, wahoo, and sailfish.

Surfcasting

Surfcasting is a shore-based fishing method where anglers cast their lines from sandy beaches or rocky shorelines into the surf. It allows for targeting fish that venture close to the shoreline to feed.

- **Equipment:**

Surfcasting requires a long fishing rod (usually 9-13 feet) for casting distance, a strong reel with a large line capacity, sinkers or weights to keep the bait anchored, and various bait options such as cut bait, shellfish, or artificial lures.

- **Techniques:**

Anglers cast their bait or lure into the breaking waves, allowing them to drift in the current. By varying casting distances and locations, anglers can target different species and adjust their techniques based on tide and surf conditions.

- **Target Species:**

Surfcasting is commonly used for catching species such as

snapper, kahawai, kingfish, tailor, and various flatfish species.

Longlining

Longlining is a commercial fishing method that involves deploying a long mainline with multiple baited hooks suspended at regular intervals. The mainline can extend for several miles and is left in the water for a period of time to catch fish.

- **Equipment:**

Longlining requires a commercial fishing vessel equipped with hydraulic or mechanical longline systems, a mainlineconsisting of a durable fishing line, hooks, bait, and buoys or markers to locate and retrieve the line.

- **Techniques:**

The longline is set at specific depths and locations known to have target fish species. The hooks are baited with natural or artificial bait and spaced apart along the mainline. Once the set time has elapsed, the long line is hauled in, and the catch is harvested.

- **Target Species:**

Longlining targets a wide range of species depending on the location and fishing regulations. Common targets include tuna, swordfish, halibut, snapper, and various deep-sea fish.

Jigging

Jigging is a fishing technique involving a jig, a type of lure that is repeatedly jerked or moved vertically in the water to imitate a wounded or darting prey fish. This method is known for its versatility and effectiveness in attracting predatory fish.

- **Equipment:**

Jigging requires a specialized jigging rod, a high-speed reel with a strong drag system, and a selection of jigs in various sizes, weights, and colors.

- **Techniques:**

Anglers drop the jig into the water and manipulate it with rhythmic up-and-down or jerking motions to mimic the movement of injured baitfish. Jigging can be done from a boat or shore, targeting different depths and structures where fish are likely to be present.

- **Target Species:**

Target species for jigging include tuna, kingfish, mahi-mahi, Spanish mackerel, snapper, grouper, cod, amberjack, sailfish, wahoo, barracuda, and amber.

Freshwater Fishing Methods

Freshwater fishing includes the following methods:

Fly Fishing

Fly fishing is a method that involves using a specialized fly rod, reel, and artificial flies made of feathers, fur, and other materials. It is characterized by delicate presentations and imitating the insects or baitfish that fish feed on.

- **Equipment:**

Fly fishing requires a fly rod, fly reel, fly line, and various flies. Anglers also use accessories like leaders, tippets, and fly boxes to store their flies.

- **Techniques:**

Fly fishing involves casting the fly line and flying to specific spots on the water surface, mimicking the natural movement of insects or baitfish. The angler uses various casting techniques, including the overhead cast, roll cast, and mending, to present the fly in a lifelike manner.

- **Target Species:**

Fly fishing is popular for targeting trout, salmon, bass, pan fish, and other freshwater species known for their selective feeding habits.

Spin Fishing

Spin fishing is a versatile and accessible method that uses a spinning rod and reel combination to cast and retrieve lures or bait. It is known for its ease of use and versatility in covering different water depths and conditions.

- **Equipment:**

Spin fishing requires a spinning rod, spinning reel, fishing line, and a variety of lures or bait options. Spinners, spoons, soft plastics, and crankbaits are common lures used in spin fishing.

- **Techniques:**

Spin fishing involves casting the lure or bait and retrieving it through the water using a combination of reeling and rod movements. Anglers can use different retrieval speeds, pauses, and jerks to entice strikes from fish.

- **Target Species:**

Spin fishing is effective for a wide range of freshwater species, including trout, bass, pike, walleye, pan fish, and even larger species like Muskie and catfish.

Bait Fishing

Bait fishing, or bait casting or bottom fishing, involves using natural or artificial bait to attract and catch fish. It is a traditional and straightforward method commonly used by anglers of all skill levels.

- **Equipment:**

Bait fishing requires a fishing rod, reel, fishing line, hooks, and various types of baits, such as worms, minnows, insects, or prepared baits.

- **Techniques:**

Bait fishing involves rigging the bait onto the hook and casting it into the water. The bait can be suspended at a desired depth using weights or allowed to rest on the bottom. Anglers may use techniques like still fishing, drift fishing, or bottom bouncing, depending on the target species and fishing conditions.

- **Target Species:**

Bait fishing can be effective for various freshwater species, including trout, catfish, carp, perch, sunfish, and many others.

Each freshwater fishing method offers unique experiences and opportunities to target species in lakes, rivers, and streams. Anglers can choose the method that best suits their preferences and their specific fishing conditions.

When planning a fishing trip to New Zealand, engaging with reputable outfitters ensures visitors can make the most of their time, increase their chances of success, and have a memorable fishing adventure in the country's breathtaking natural landscapes.

Benefits of Fishing in New Zealand

Some of the benefits of fishing include:

Health Benefits
Exercise:

Fishing involves physical activity such as casting, reeling, and maneuvering while on boats or wading in water. It can provide moderate exercise, promoting cardiovascular health, muscle strength, and coordination.

Stress Relief:

Fishing offers an opportunity to disconnect from daily routines, reduce stress, and relax in natural surroundings. The calm and peaceful environment and the rhythmic nature of fishing can have a therapeutic effect on the mind and body.

Mindfulness and Relaxation:

Fishing encourages mindfulness as anglers focus on the present moment, the movements of the rod and line, and the sensations of the environment. It can help reduce anxiety, improve mental clarity, and promote well-being.

Connection to Nature:

Fishing allows individuals to immerse themselves in the natural beauty of New Zealand's lakes, rivers, and coastlines. It fosters a deeper connection to nature, appreciation for the environment, and a sense of tranquility.

Economic Benefits

Tourism:

Fishing in New Zealand attracts both domestic and international tourists, contributing to the country's tourism industry. Anglers travel to various regions to pursue their favorite fishing experiences, stimulating local economies through accommodation, dining, and other tourism-related expenditures.

Job Opportunities:

Fishing-related activities support a range of employment opportunities in New Zealand. This includes guides, outfitters, charter operators, boat rentals, tackle shops, hospitality services, and more. The fishing industry generates income and sustains livelihoods for many individuals.

Environmental Benefits
Sustainable Fishing Practices:

New Zealand is known for its commitment to sustainable fishing practices. By adhering to regulations and guidelines, anglers contribute to conserving and preserving fish populations and their habitats. Sustainable fishing helps maintain the ecological balance of aquatic ecosystems and ensures the longevity of fish stocks for future generations.

Conservation Efforts:

Fishing communities and organizations in New Zealand actively engage in conservation efforts, including habitat restoration, fish stocking programs, and environmental education. These initiatives contribute to protecting and preserving natural resources and promoting a sustainable fishing environment.

By recognizing and promoting the various benefits of fishing in New Zealand, individuals and communities can appreciate this activity's holistic value, encompassing physical health, mental well-being, economic growth, and environmental stewardship.

Responsible Fishing Actions

If someone from outside of New Zealand is planning to pursue fishing in the country, there are several steps they can take to ensure a smooth and enjoyable fishing experience:

Research Fishing Regulations

It is essential to familiarize yourself with the fishing regulations and licensing requirements in New Zealand. Different regions may have specific rules and restrictions regarding bag limits, size limits, fishing seasons, and permitted fishing methods. The New Zealand government's official fisheries website provides comprehensive information on fishing regulations.

Obtain the Necessary Licenses

Depending on the type of fishing and location, anglers may need to obtain fishing licenses. Licenses can be obtained online through the New Zealand Fish & Game website or from local fishing and outdoor stores.

Seek Local Knowledge

New Zealand offers diverse fishing opportunities, and local knowledge is invaluable for finding the best fishing spots, understanding local conditions, and targeting specific species. Connecting with local fishing clubs, forums, or experienced anglers can provide insights and recommendations.

Engage with Outfitters

Outfitters play a crucial role in helping visitors make the most of their fishing experiences in New Zealand. These professionals have extensive knowledge of local waters and fishing techniques and can provide equipment, boats, and transportation services. They can tailor fishing trips based on skill levels, preferences, and desired target species. Outfitters also offer guided fishing tours, providing a hassle-free and immersive fishing experience.

Role of Outfitters

The role of outfitters in helping visitors to New Zealand is significant. They offer the following benefits:

Local Expertise

Outfitters have in-depth knowledge of the local fishing areas, including the best spots, productive times, and effective techniques for targeting specific species. They can provide guidance on fishing regulations and ensure visitors comply with legal requirements.

Equipment and Gear

Outfitters typically provide all the necessary fishing equipment, gear, and bait, saving visitors the hassle of bringing or purchasing their own gear. They ensure anglers are equipped with appropriate rods, reels, lines, lures, and other fishing essentials.

Safety and Convenience

Fishing outfitters prioritize safety and provide a comfortable and convenient experience. They often offer transportation services, arrange fishing licenses, and handle logistics such as boat rentals, accommodations, and meals.

Learning Opportunities

Fishing outfitters can provide valuable insights and

techniques, helping visitors improve their fishing skills and knowledge. They may offer casting, baiting, and landing fish instructions, making the experience educational and enjoyable.

The best way for tourists to make the most of their time, improve their odds of catching fish, and have an unforgettable fishing excursion in New Zealand's stunning natural settings is to work with respected outfitters. These outfitters will guide you through the ropes and help you make the most of your hunting experience out there in "The Land Down Under."

In a nutshell, we embarked on a fishing journey in New Zealand and learned about its historical significance, diverse fishing methods, and numerous benefits of fishing.

We explored sea fishing methods such as trolling, surfcasting, longlining, and jigging and freshwater fishing methods like fly fishing, spin fishing, and bait fishing. Additionally, we gained insights into the rich Maori cultural connections to fishing and how it is deeply woven into their traditions.

The chapter emphasized the physical, mental, economic, and environmental advantages of fishing, underscoring the importance of responsible and sustainable fishing practices.

Furthermore, we also learned that in order to ensure a fantastic fishing experience, outfitters play a crucial role by guiding anglers, ensuring compliance with regulations, and fostering responsible fishing practices.

In summary, tourists are encouraged to embrace responsible fishing practices, collaborate with outfitters, and actively contribute to preserving New Zealand's stunning aquatic environments.

Chapter 11
Fishing Basics and Gears

In this chapter, you will learn some basic fishing concepts and the importance of understanding these basics before heading out for a fishing adventure in New Zealand.

Understanding Fishing: A Brief Overview

Fishing is an ancient practice that crosses cultures and geographical boundaries. It could be a survival skill, a career, a sport, or a calming hobby. The thrill of the quest, the patience it instills, the connection it forms with nature, and the satisfaction of catching a fish are what make this game a next-level experience.

To those unfamiliar with the sport, fishing may appear to be as simple as tossing a line into the water and waiting for a fish to bite. While this is the fundamental premise, good fishing entails a succession of well-executed actions. It all starts with studying the species of fish in a particular body of water and selecting the necessary gear. Knowledge of the fish's feeding habits, time of day, and meteorological conditions are other important considerations. Once on the water, anglers must cast their lines expertly, retain a keen eye and feel for strikes, and then hook and reel in the fish without losing it. It's a sequence that needs both skill and calm, producing a one-of-a-kind and satisfying challenge.

The beauty of fishing is found in its variety. You can go fishing in a small brook, a big ocean, a teeming river, or even beneath a thick sheet of ice. This gives rise to various sorts of fishing, each with its own set of obstacles and rewards.

Freshwater Fishing entails catching fish in bodies of water such as lakes, rivers, ponds, or streams. Bass, catfish, and trout may be found here. Freshwater fishing is a great place to start for beginners, with tactics that can be as simple or as complicated as you choose.

Saltwater Fishing is typically associated with ocean fishing. This can happen on the beach (surf fishing), on a boat (offshore or inshore fishing), or even on a pier. Saltwater fish species range in size from little mackerel to huge marlins.

Fly Fishing is a distinct and artistic kind of fishing in which a lightweight lure (called a fly) is used to catch fish. This style, which is noted for its aesthetic appeal, necessitates a unique casting technique. Fly fishing is commonly used to catch trout and salmon, but the technique may be employed to catch a wide range of species.

Ice Fishing entails fishing through a hole in the ice of a frozen lake or pond. Despite the difficult conditions, this type of fishing may be thrilling and necessitates specific equipment.

Each type of fishing presents its own set of obstacles and rewards. Saltwater fishing, for example, can yield larger catches but requires more power and experience. Freshwater fishing may necessitate a greater understanding of fish behavior and water currents. Fly fishing necessitates learning the art of casting, whereas ice fishing tests the angler's cold tolerance and patience.

Fishing, regardless of the form, is a meaningful way to engage with nature, delivering a sense of tranquility and accomplishment that draws millions of enthusiasts worldwide.

Why Should You Go Fishing in New Zealand?

New Zealand is a fishing enthusiast's paradise, a place where anglers can pursue their love amid some of the world's most breathtaking scenery. Here are five reasons why fishing in New Zealand is an unforgettable experience.

For starters, the country's geographical features offer a plethora of various fishing places. New Zealand has over 15,000 kilometers of shoreline, not to mention a plethora of freshwater bodies such as lakes, rivers, and streams that cut across picturesque landscapes. There are numerous fishing sites that accommodate every angler's preference, from the turquoise waters of Lake Tekapo to the rich seas of the Bay of Islands. Whether you enjoy peaceful freshwater fly-fishing or the adrenaline rush of battling a large game fish at sea, New Zealand has it all.

The pristine and diverse ecosystems of New Zealand, where conservation and appreciation for the environment are strongly embedded in the country's culture, add to this attractiveness. New Zealand's fisheries management system is highly regarded around the world, with sustainable methods ensuring that diverse marine and freshwater habitats continue to thrive. This ensures not just a plethora of fish today but also abundant fishing possibilities for future generations.

New Zealand is home to a diverse range of fish species that would pique the interest of any angler. Freshwater bodies are overflowing with world-class rainbow and brown trout, as well as sizable salmon populations. Snapper, Kingfish, and even the renowned Marlin can be found in the saltwater, providing a fantastic game fishing experience.

But the fishing experience in New Zealand is much more than just the catch. It's about immersing oneself in the breathtaking, calm settings that make fishing here a spiritual as well as a physical experience. Anglers in New Zealand are completely engaged in the magnificence of nature, whether they are surrounded by lush foliage, snow-capped mountains, or stunning cliffs falling into the sea.

Finally, professional fishing services in New Zealand provide everything from equipment rental to guided tours, ensuring that both novice and experienced fishermen get the most out of their fishing experience. Full-service outfitting companies like to make fishing excursions in New Zealand simple, entertaining, and successful. They assist you in traversing the amazing waterways of New Zealand, targeting the best areas and assuring a memorable and gratifying journey using local expertise, adequate gear, and top-notch guiding.

Finally, fishing in New Zealand provides a one-of-a-kind combination of magnificent scenery, different fish species, sustainable practices, and high-quality professional services. It's a must-visit for any angler, promising an experience that extends beyond the excitement of the catch.

Common Fish Types in New Zealand

New Zealand has many different water ecosystems that are home to various types of fish. Here are some of the most popular types of fish that fishermen in New Zealand target:

Freshwater Fish

Rainbow Trout

Rainbow trout is one of the most popular freshwater fishing species. Rainbow Trout are exciting to catch because of their striking, vivid patterns and intense fighting attitude. They live in a wide range of freshwater settings, including pristine mountain streams and vast, muddy lakes.

Brown Trout

Brown trout are prevalent in rivers and streams throughout New Zealand. Fly fishers admire them for their selectiveness and wariness, which makes them a difficult but rewarding catch. Brown trout are highly prized for their stunning golden-brown coloring and enormous size.

Chinook Salmon

Chinook Salmon, sometimes known as King Salmon, are the largest salmon species and can be found in a few rivers in the South Island. They are most plentiful during the yearly salmon run in late summer and are in high demand because of their size and the richness of their flesh.

Saltwater Fish

Snapper

Snappers are the most popular saltwater fish among New Zealand recreational fishermen, especially in the warmer northern waters. They are prized for their succulent meat and can be caught all year. However, summer is the most popular season.

Kingfish

These fierce fighters, sometimes known as Yellowtail Kingfish, are highly prized by sport fishermen. They can be found in rocky places and around offshore islands, and their strength and speed are known to present fishermen with tremendous challenges.

Blue Cod

Blue cod are a popular catch for South Island fishers. They are recognized for their beautiful blue color and delicate, tasty flesh and can be found in rocky, weedy environments.

Each of these species presents its own set of challenges and rewards, and understanding their behavior and habitats will vastly improve your fishing experience in New Zealand.

Essential Gear for Fishing

Having the proper equipment might mean the difference between a successful and a disappointing day on the lake. Here's a rundown of the basic fishing equipment you'll need for a thrilling and productive fishing experience in New Zealand.

Rods

An angler's principal tool is the fishing rod. Rods are available in a range of sizes and styles, each tailored to a particular sort of fishing or species. Lightweight rods are often used for freshwater fishing or pursuing lesser saltwater species, and larger rods are ideal for ocean big-game fishing. Always select a rod that is appropriate for the style of fishing you intend to undertake and the species you hope to catch.

Reels

The fishing reel is attached to the rod and has two functions: it stores your fishing line and helps you cast and retrieve it. Spinning reels, baitcasting reels, and fly reels are the three basic types of fishing reels. Each type of reel has its own set of applications and qualities, and your choice is determined by your level of experience and the type of fishing you intend to conduct.

Lines

The fishing line is the link between you and the fish. Fishing lines, like rods and reels, come in a variety of styles. Monofilament lines are popular among novices since they are versatile and simple to use. Underwater, fluorocarbon lines are nearly undetectable, while braided lines are noted for their strength. The line you use will be determined by the fishing environment and the species you are pursuing.

Hooks

The hook is the piece of equipment used to catch the fish. Hooks are available in a variety of sizes and shapes. Some hooks are intended to be concealed within the bait, while others are intended to be used with artificial lures. The size and type of hook you require will be determined by the species you are targeting and the sort of bait you are using.

Lures and Baits

Bait is what draws fish to your hook. Baits can be live (such as worms or minnows), dead (such as cut fish parts), or artificial (lures). The bait or lure you use can have a significant impact on your success and is generally determined by what the fish in your particular location are known to eat.

Fishing Tackle Container

A tackle box is where you keep all of your fishing equipment, such as hooks, lines, sinkers, lures, pliers, a first aid kit, and so on. A well-organized tackle box can improve the efficiency and enjoyment of your fishing excursion.

Different Types of Fishing Gear (Freshwater vs. Saltwater)

Certain types of fishing may necessitate the use of specialized equipment. Fly fishing, for example, necessitates the use of a specifically constructed rod, reel, and artificial flies. Saltwater fishing may necessitate corrosion-resistant equipment, but fishing for larger species may necessitate stronger, more durable equipment.

Remember that having the appropriate equipment can dramatically improve your fishing experience and raise your chances of success. Always choose equipment that is suited to your skill level, the fishing conditions, and the species you want to catch. Finally, regular equipment care and maintenance will ensure its longevity and performance. The diverse fishing settings of New Zealand provide multiple opportunities to test various gear and techniques, making each fishing excursion a unique adventure.

Appropriate Fishing Clothing and Accessories

Aside from fishing equipment, it is critical to dress adequately for a fishing expedition. The correct apparel may keep you safe from the weather, increase your comfort, and even improve your fishing efficiency. Here are some crucial clothes and accessory items to consider:

Weather-Responsive Clothing

You should wear layers depending on the time of year and the weather. You can then add or remove garments as desired. Always keep an eye on the forecast and plan accordingly. For rainy days, waterproof coats and trousers are needed, and insulating apparel is essential for chilly weather. To stay comfortable on hot, sunny days, use lightweight, breathable, and moisture-wicking fabrics.

Fisherman's Vest

Anglers might benefit from a fishing vest because it is both adaptable and functional. It has many pockets and compartments for convenient access to your regularly used fishing equipment, such as lures, hooks, lines, and pliers. This can save you time and improve the efficiency of your fishing experience.

Sunglasses and Hats

A good hat will keep the sun off your face and neck while also reducing glare off the water, making it easier to sight fish. Sunglasses, particularly polarized ones, protect your eyes from dangerous UV rays and reduce water glare, making it easier to identify fish.

Water-Resistant Footwear

You're going to get your feet wet while fishing, whether you're standing on a boat, walking along a riverbank, or wading in the water. Water-resistant boots or waders will keep your feet dry and comfy. Non-slip soles are also useful since they can avoid slips on damp, slippery surfaces.

Personal Flotation Device (PFD)

When you're on or near the water, safety comes first. A PFD, or life jacket, is required while fishing from a boat or wading in deep or fast-moving water. Even experienced swimmers might get into problems in the water, so don't ignore this important piece of safety equipment.

The appropriate gear and clothes can make your fishing excursion safer, more pleasant, and more successful. Dress appropriately for the weather, think about functional clothing like a fishing vest, cover your feet and eyes, and always emphasize safety with a PFD. Fishing in New Zealand's surroundings might provide unique challenges, but with the proper gear, you can fully appreciate everything these breathtaking fishing places have to offer.

Transportation and Lodging for Fishing Trips

Planning your transportation and lodging is an important element of any fishing trip. Having the right vehicle and all of the required supplies for an overnight stay will greatly improve your fishing experience.

Choosing an Appropriate Vehicle for Fishing Trips

The vehicle you select for your fishing excursion should meet your requirements for comfort, spaciousness, and accessibility. If you intend to fish in isolated areas or on rough terrain, a 4WD vehicle will help you travel effectively. Make sure your car has enough room for all of your gear as well as any other fisherman. Roof racks or trailers can be useful for transporting heavier goods such as boats or heavy equipment.

Breakdowns in isolated regions might be difficult if the vehicle is not trustworthy and in good shape. In case of a flat tire or small repairs, always keep a spare tire, jack, and basic tools on hand.

Overnight Fishing Trip Essentials

When planning an overnight fishing excursion, make sure

you prepare correctly for comfort and safety. Here are some crucial items to think about:

Camper Trailer or Tent

A tent or camper trailer, depending on your preferences and the number of people, can give you a comfortable place to sleep and shelter from the weather. Make sure it's simple to set up and take down.

Sleeping Bag or Mattress

A good quality sleeping bag that is appropriate for the forecasted temperatures is essential. A sleeping mat or air mattress might provide additional comfort.

Cooking Supplies

Portable burners, pots, and utensils are required for meal preparation. Don't forget about the stove fuel.

Food and Drink

Pack enough food to last the duration of your vacation, plus some extra for emergencies. Carry adequate water with you at all times, especially in distant areas where it may not be readily available.

Lighting

Headlamps or torches are required for nighttime navigation.

A lantern can also be used to light up your campground.

First-Aid Kit

On any fishing trip, a well-stocked first-aid kit is a requirement. Bandages, antiseptic wipes, tweezers, painkillers, and other personal medication you may require should be included.

Emergency Provisions

Depending on where you're going and how long you'll be gone, you might want to bring a compass, map, multi-tool, fire-starting kit, and a whistle or other signaling device.

Planning and preparation beforehand can help to ensure a good fishing excursion. From selecting the correct vehicle to packing all of the necessary equipment for an overnight stay, these procedures will help you to enjoy the unique and different fishing experiences that New Zealand has to offer.

Using an outfitter may substantially ease the process of booking transportation and lodging for your fishing trip in New Zealand. Being industry veterans, they can offer a fleet of dependable and terrain-appropriate cars that are properly maintained and outfitted with roof racks or trailers for your stuff. This not only provides comfortable and safe travel to your fishing spot, but it also reduces the burden of vehicle rental and wear and tear on your own vehicle.

You save time and energy with the help of an outfitter, allowing you to maximize your fishing time and fully immerse yourself in the wonderful New Zealand environment. Furthermore, you benefit from their comprehensive local expertise about the finest fishing places, conditions, and techniques, which can considerably improve your chances of catching a fish.

Skills Required for Fishing

Fishing is a sport that necessitates a combination of abilities, patience, and knowledge. Whether you're a beginner or an experienced angler, developing these abilities will make your fishing experience more fruitful and enjoyable.

Casting Methods

Casting is a key skill in fishing. The ability to correctly put your lure or bait at the proper distance can dramatically boost your chances of catching fish. Various fishing strategies necessitate distinct casting techniques, such as overhead casting, roll casting, or side casting.

Overhead Cast

This is the most common casting technique, sometimes known as the two-handed overhand cast. The angler draws the rod back over their shoulder and swings it forward fluidly, releasing the line at the precise moment to send the bait or lure flying toward the target.

Roll Cast

The roll cast includes swinging the rod forward without first pulling it back. It is useful in situations where there is limited room behind you. It's a common fly-fishing technique.

Side Cast

This method includes casting the line to the side rather than overhead, which is advantageous in windy situations or in small locations.

Types of Knots and Learning When to Use Them

Another important skill in fishing is knot-tying. The proper knot can spell the difference between landing a large fish and letting it swim away. The Improved Clinch Knot, Palomar Knot, and Loop Knot are three of the most frequent fishing knots, each providing a different purpose.

Improved Clinch Knot

This is a common knot used to secure a fishing line to a hook, lure, or swivel. It's robust, dependable, and simple to knot.

Palomar Knot

The Palomar knot, known for its strength and simplicity, is ideal for fastening your line to a hook or lure, especially when using braided fishing lines.

Knot Loop

This knot forms a loop that allows the hook or lures to move freely, making it great for giving your lure a more natural action.

Hooking and Hook Setting

Knowing how to correctly set the hook after a fish bite keeps it from escaping. This needs a combination of timing, speed, and force, which varies according to the sort of fish you're attempting to catch.

Fish Catching

Once you have hooked a fish, you must know how to land it. This is frequently the most difficult stage of the fight and the point at which many fish are lost. Controlling the fish, maintaining line tension, and efficiently using your rod and reel are all necessary skills. Having an outfitter with you at such points will assist you throughout the procedure, ensuring a successful capture.

Releasing Fish Properly

Knowing how to handle and release the fish correctly is critical for its survival if you practice catch and release. It is critical to keep the fish out of the water for as little time as possible, to handle it gently, and to guarantee that it is revived before releasing it.

Navigation and Safety Knowledge

It is vital to be able to find your fishing site, understand weather trends, and stay safe on the water. This involves learning how to use a compass or GPS, tides and currents (for saltwater fishing), and basic water safety guidelines.

While fishing is a calm and fun hobby, it also necessitates a specific set of abilities to be effective. You'll be able to learn and hone these abilities with the help of an outfitter service, increasing your chances of a profitable catch and assuring a safe and pleasurable time in New Zealand's magnificent waters.

Preparing Your Catch

After successfully landing your catch, the next step is to prepare it. This section will walk you through the entire process, from cleaning and gutting your catch to preparing or preserving it.

Fish Cleaning and Gutting

The initial steps in preparing your catch for food are cleaning and gutting. It entails removing the fish's scales, gills, and internal organs, leaving only the edible parts. This procedure assures that the fish is safe to consume while also improving its flavor.

Filleting Methods

Filleting is a method of removing the bones from a fish to get a flat piece of fish meat. The procedure varies slightly depending on the type and size of fish, but in general, it entails creating an incision behind the gills and cutting along the backbone to the tail.

Fish Preservation: On Ice vs. Smoking

If you're not going to consume your catch right away, properly preserving it is critical. The most usual way is to keep the fish on ice. It entails placing the fish in an ice-filled cooler to keep it fresh until you're ready to cook it.

Smoking, on the other hand, is a traditional method of preserving fish that also imparts a distinct flavor. It entails bringing the fish in salt and then smoking it over an open fire.

Basic Cooking Recipes for Your Catch

The final prize of your fishing excursion is cooking your catch. We can share some simple and delicious dishes that bring out the greatest tastes of the fish, whether you prefer grilling, frying, baking, or cooking a stew.

Catch and Release Ethics: When to Keep and When to Release

While it's fun to keep and cook your catch, it's also crucial to practice ethical fishing by knowing when to release a fish. This could be because it's a protected species, it's smaller than the legal-size limit, or you've already caught your daily bag limit. Catch and release also contribute to the preservation of fish populations for future generations of anglers. Professional outfitters are devoted to encouraging ethical fishing techniques and will educate you on local legislation and catch and release procedures.

Preparing your catch is an important aspect of the fishing experience, as it gives you a sense of accomplishment and appreciation for the sport. With an outfitter's help, you'll learn how to responsibly handle your catch, whether that means cooking it for a meal or returning it to the water.

In a nutshell, fishing is more than just a sport or a hobby in New Zealand. It's an opportunity to reconnect with nature, relax, challenge yourself, and even enjoy the excitement of the catch.

By learning the information in this book, you'll be ready for your next fishing trip in New Zealand. But real knowledge comes from having lived through things. So, dive into the exciting world of fishing: enjoy the thrill of casting your line into the clear waters, enjoy the excitement of waiting for a bite, enjoy the joy of reeling in your catch, and enjoy the satisfaction of preparing your own haul. Ultimately, choose a skilled and experienced guide who can improve your fishing trip and make it easier to enjoy.

Chapter 12
Attributes of New Zealand's
Fisheries Landscape

Welcome to Aotearoa, also known as New Zealand or the Land of the Long White Cloud. This little but mighty country in the South Pacific boasts an incredible array of landscapes, from towering mountain ranges to peaceful beaches, lush rainforests, and all in between. It is a natural playground and an angler's paradise.

The terrain of New Zealand provides a unique combination of temperate and subtropical climates, resulting in a diverse range of maritime ecosystems. The junction of the Tasman Sea and the Pacific Ocean contributes to a rich, biodiverse marine life, providing an incredible diversity of fishing opportunities not found anywhere else on the planet.

The Rich Biodiversity of New Zealand Waters

The oceans around New Zealand are teeming with life. With over 15,000 kilometers of shoreline and several lakes, rivers, and streams, these waterways are home to an incredible diversity of creatures. New Zealand caters to all types of fishermen, from migratory game fish like marlin, swordfish, and yellowfin tuna in deeper ocean seas to coveted trout and salmon in freshwater rivers and lakes.

For saltwater anglers, New Zealand's wide coastlineprovides several possibilities to capture snapper, kingfish, and hapuka. Rivers and lakes offer some of the best trout and salmon fishing in the world, with big populations of both rainbow and brown trout.

The Cultural Importance of Fishing in New Zealand

Fishing is more than a recreational pastime in New Zealand; it is an intrinsic component of the country's identity. This passion for fishing can be traced back to the Mori, New Zealand's indigenous people. The Mori have a close relationship with the water, seeing it as a source of sustenance and a route to new regions. These ancient beliefs have been passed down through generations, affecting modern fishing techniques in New Zealand.

The fishing heritage is also represented in New Zealand's conservation efforts. The country recognizes the value of preserving a sustainable fishing environment, which fishermen will notice through rules and license requirements meant to safeguard and preserve these distinct aquatic ecosystems.

Whether you're casting a line from a gorgeous beach, going deep sea fishing, or fly fishing in a crystal-clear stream surrounded by majestic mountains, New Zealand provides an exceptional fishing experience that extends beyond the pleasure of the catch. Immersing yourself in a rich cultural tradition and magnificently diverse natural scenery that takes your breath away at every turn is what it's all about.

The North Island: A Fisherman's Paradise

The North Island of New Zealand, known as Te Ika-a-Mui in Mori, is a paradise for fishermen. There is no shortage of opportunities for spectacular fishing adventures, from the thriving saltwater fisheries of the coast to the trout-laden freshwater rivers and lakes.

Locating the Best Fishing Spots

The North Island of New Zealand, with its broad coastline, crystal-clear lakes, and rushing rivers, provides a diverse range of fishing opportunities. Each location offers a distinct blend of natural beauty and fish species, ensuring not only a good catch but also a beautiful connection with nature. Whether you're casting off the beach, joining a deep-sea fishing charter, or navigating the currents of a freshwater stream, you're sure to find an ideal fishing place that will transform your vacation into an amazing fishing excursion.

Some of the best fishing spots on the North Island are:

Islands Bay

The Bay of Islands, being one of New Zealand's most popular tourist locations, provides an outstanding saltwater fishing experience. A variety of species, including snapper, kingfish, and even marlin, are drawn to the subtropical climate.

Lake Taupo

As New Zealand's largest lake, Lake Taupo is a trout fishing heaven. The lake is stocked with rainbow and brown trout, and while they are difficult to catch, the rewards are well worth the effort, with trout averaging 3-4 pounds.

The Peninsula of Coromandel

The Coromandel Peninsula, known for its natural beauty, is also a popular spot for saltwater fishing. The main goals are snapper and kingfish but don't neglect the possibility of catching John Dory and Trevally.

Manukau Harbour

As New Zealand's second-largest harbor, Manukau Harbour offers a unique fishing experience. Snapper, flounder, and even the rare gurnard can be found here.

Waikato River

New Zealand's longest river is another great site for trout fishing. River tributaries such as the Tongariro, Tauranga-Taupo, and Waitahanui are also extremely productive.

Identifying Important Fish Species

The waterways of the North Island are filled with a plethora of fish species, each with its own set of challenges and rewards. These different fish species cater to a wide spectrum of fishing interests, from those who appreciate the adrenaline rush of battling a strong marlin in the open ocean to others who find tranquility in the painstaking art of fly fishing for trout in a tranquil river. Recognizing the local fish species will enhance your fishing experience by allowing you to modify your approach and anticipate the fight of the fish on your line.

Let's get started identifying some of the important species you'll see in the seas of the North Island.

Snapper

Snapper, New Zealand's most popular sportfish, is abundant throughout the North Island. These formidable fighters can be found in a range of environments, including rocky reefs, sandy bottoms, and around structures.

Kingfish

Known for their battling spirit, kingfish are another popular target for North Island saltwater fishermen. Because they are drawn to buildings, search for them around reefs, wharves, and mussel farms.

Rainbow and Brown Trout

Both of these freshwater species can be found in a variety of rivers and lakes throughout the North Island, although Lake Taupo and the Waikato River are particularly abundant.

Marlin

While not as frequent as snapper or trout, marlin is a sought-after catch for deep-sea fishermen. The Bay of Islands is a great area to try your luck at catching these spectacular billfish.

The numerous fishing areas and species on the North Island provide a limitless number of options for great fishing adventures. Whether you're a seasoned angler or a novice, the North Island is sure to have a fishing trip to suit you.

The South Island: Anglers' Paradise

The South Island of New Zealand, known as Te Waipounamu in Mori, provides a fascinating contrast to the fishing destinations of the North Island. The South Island is known for its pristine scenery, which ranges from lofty alpine ranges to untamed southern coasts. It's a haven for fishermen seeking a deeper connection with nature while throwing a line.

Exploring Prime Fishing Spots

South Island fishing offers a plethora of opportunities to encounter diverse and rich marine life. Each place has its own unique scenery and species, guaranteeing a scenic as well as fruitful experience.

Fiordland

Fiordland, known for its sheer cliffs and deep waters, is an excellent location for marine fishing. Anglers frequently catch blue cod, groper, and trumpeter here.

The Nelson Lakes

Nelson Lakes National Park is a great place to go freshwater fishing. Brown and rainbow trout can be found in abundance here.

Kaikoura

Kaikoura is well known for its crayfish, but it also offers good marine fishing. Groper, blue cod, and sea perch are among the species present in this area.

The Otago Peninsula

Blue cod, sea perch, and groper are frequently found in these waters, making this an excellent area for both shore and boat fishing.

Each of these spots offers its own set of thrills and difficulties, offering an amazing fishing trip.

Identifying Diverse Fish Species in South Island

Fishing in the South Island's different water settings allows you to interact with a wide variety of creatures. Recognizing these species and comprehending their behavior can give you an advantage in catching your intended catch.

Rainbow and Brown Trout

These species are the highlight of South Island freshwater fishing, with Nelson Lakes and other rivers, such as the Mataura River, serving as their preferred habitats.

Cape Cod

The blue cod is a favorite among sea anglers due to its exquisite taste and availability in the South Island's coastal waters.

Groper

This species, also known as Hpuku, is a highly sought-after target due to its size and the quality of its flesh. They are typically found in deeper water.

The Sea Perch

These species are common in coastal locations between Kaikoura and the Otago Peninsula, providing fishermen with a reliable catch.

Trumpeter

Anglers admire these remarkable fish for their size and gastronomic appeal, which are frequently found in Fiordland.

All in all, the South Island provides an enormous array of fishing chances that are difficult to duplicate. The breathtaking scenery provides a tranquil backdrop for any fishing expedition, and the richness and variety of fish species cater to all sorts of fishermen. Whether you prefer fishing in a calm lake or a raging sea, the South Island has something for everyone. The South Island is an angler's paradise because of the thrill of the catch paired with the calm of the gorgeous natural landscape.

Learning about Licenses and Regulations

Before you may cast a line into New Zealand's seas, you must first understand the legalities and procedures. Compliance with these standards is about more than just avoiding penalties or fines; it's about contributing to the long-term viability of the country's various aquatic ecosystems.

This section will walk you through the license application process, provide an introduction to fishing regulations, and emphasize the importance of conservation and ethical fishing practices.

Navigating the License Acquisition Process

Different fishing licenses are necessary in New Zealand for sea and freshwater fishing. A license is not required for saltwater fishing unless you are spearfishing or harvesting shellfish. However, a license is required for freshwater fishing, notably for trout and salmon.

Freshwater Fishing License

Freshwater fishing is managed by the New Zealand Fish & Game Council. Permits are available for purchase on the Fish & Game website, and there are a range of options available, ranging from whole-season permits to one-day licenses catering to both locals and non-residents.

Shellfish and Spearfishing License

The Ministry of Primary Industries (MPI) is in charge of shellfish and spearfishing licenses. More information about the process and fees can be found on the MPI's website.

Fishing Regulations Unpacked

Fishing rules in New Zealand vary according to region and species. Bag limits, size restrictions, fishing methods, and protected species are all covered by these regulations. Here's a quick rundown:

Saltwater Fishing Regulations

The regulations for saltwater fishing include daily bag limits and minimum size requirements for several species. These differ by region, so check the MPI's rules for the exact area where you'll be fishing.

Freshwater Fishing Rules

Freshwater fishing in New Zealand is world-renowned,

notably for trout and salmon. However, in order to preserve these world-class fisheries for future generations, the country has enacted a set of rules and restrictions that all anglers must follow. Fish & Game New Zealand is in charge of these rules, which vary by location. As a result, it's critical to become acquainted with the guidelines for the specific location where you'll be fishing. Here's a high-level overview:

Fishing Seasons

The freshwater fishing season normally runs from October 1 to April 30, though this might vary based on region and body of water. Some regions may have an open season all year, while others may be limited during certain times of the year to protect spawning salmon.

Daily Bag and Size Limits

There are rigorous limits in place governing the number of fish you can retain each day (bag limit) and the minimum size of these fish. Again, these rules can vary widely amongst regions. For example, the daily bag limit for trout in certain regions can be six, while in others, it may be as low as two. Always double-check local legislation to verify you're in line.

Approved Fishing Methods

In general, fly fishing and spinning are the only methods of freshwater fishing in New Zealand. Certain localities or bodies of water may have additional restrictions on the types of bait, hooks, or lures that can be used, so verify these regulations before heading out.

License Requirements

As previously stated, freshwater fishing requires a Fish & Game New Zealand fishing license. The sort of license you require is determined by your age, the length of time you intend to fish (season, week, or day), and whether you are a resident or visitor.

Catch and Release

To sustain healthy fish populations, catch and release is strongly promoted in New Zealand. Catch and release refers to the practice of catching a fish and then returning it to the water undamaged so that it can survive and thrive in its natural environment. Catch and release is required in several rivers and lakes, and anglers must adopt safe handling procedures to ensure the fish's survival after release.

Specific Area limits

Additional limits may apply in some areas, such as limitations on fishing near dams, in specific streams, or within designated wildlife reserves. Again, it's critical to double-check the rules for your chosen fishing spot.

These regulations are in place to safeguard the survival of New Zealand's world-class freshwater fisheries. By adhering to these laws, you are assisting in ensuring that these ecosystems stay healthy and abundant, giving outstanding angling opportunities for future generations.

Rules for Shellfish and Spearfishing

In comparison to traditional line fishing, collecting shellfish or pursuing spearfishing in New Zealand's marine waters provides an altogether distinct experience. These operations, however, are subject to their own set of rules and regulations, which are overseen by the Ministry of Primary Industries (MPI). As a tourist, you must be aware of these regulations in order to have a safe and legal fishing experience.

Shellfish Gathering

Locals and visitors alike enjoy shellfish gathering in New Zealand. However, there are several rules you must follow:

Daily Bag Limits

Each shellfish species has a daily bag restriction, which varies by area. The daily limit for green-lipped mussels, for example, is normally 50 per person per day, but always verify the MPI's standards for the individual area where you're harvesting.

Size Restrictions

Some shellfish have minimum size requirements. This protects juvenile shellfish, allowing them to reproduce and contribute to the long-term viability of the species.

Protected locations

To conserve shellfish populations, some beaches or locations may be temporarily or permanently closed to shellfish collection. Before gathering, always check local signage or the MPI website.

Spearfishing

Spearfishing is a popular recreational fishing activity in New Zealand, but it, too, has restrictions that must be followed:

License Requirement

While no special license is necessary for spearfishing, people who participate must adhere to the same fishing restrictions as line and hook fishermen. This includes observing daily bag limitations, size restrictions, and area closures.

Restricted Species

Some species are protected and cannot be caught via spearfishing. This contains, among other things, all freshwater fish, paua (a form of abalone), and marine mammals.

Equipment Restrictions

Spearfishing in New Zealand is not permitted with scuba gear or any other type of underwater breathing apparatus. The preferred and legal way is freediving.

Respect for Marine Reserves

New Zealand's marine reserves are no-take zones, and spearfishing is prohibited.

Whether you're collecting shellfish at low tide or exploring the undersea world with a spear, keep in mind that these restrictions are in place to protect New Zealand's varied marine life, ensuring it remains abundant and vibrant for future generations. It is your responsibility as a responsible tourist and angler to follow these guidelines and contribute to the continuing conservation efforts in this magnificent country.

Understanding and following New Zealand's fishing permits, rules, and conservation practices is about more than simply staying within the law; it's about respecting the magnificent aquatic ecosystems that make this country an angler's paradise.

Fishing responsibly ensures that these habitats remain rich and healthy for future generations to enjoy. The genuine spirit of fishing in New Zealand is found not only in the excitement of the catch but also in the appreciation and preservation of the country's magnificent and diverse waters.

Unraveling New Zealand Fishing Techniques

New Zealand has a diverse range of fishing experiences to offer, from the adrenaline of deep-sea fishing to the serenity of fly fishing in a pristine river. Whether you're an experienced angler or a novice, each approach has its own distinct appeal and obstacles. This section will walk you through three of New Zealand's most popular fishing techniques: deep-sea charter fishing, fly fishing, and kayak fishing.

Embracing the Exciting Adventure of Deep-Sea Charter Fishing

Exploring the deep-sea waters around New Zealand may be an exhilarating experience. Charter fishing lets you target the large game species that live in these waters, all while being guided and outfitted by professional charter crews.

The Experience

As a well-equipped boat heads out into the open sea, the anticipation grows as the depth detector locates a potential site. You never know what lurks beneath the surface when you cast your line. The potential catches are as varied as they are exciting, ranging from snapper and kingfish to marlin and tuna.

Tips and Techniques

Patience is essential when it comes to deep-sea fishing. It can take some time to find fish and even longer for them to bite. When a large fish is hooked, reeling it in can be a physical struggle that requires strength and energy.

Considerations

It is critical to select a trustworthy charter company. They should supply all necessary equipment and safety equipment, and their personnel should be well-versed in the best fishing areas and tactics.

The Fine Art of Fly Fishing

Fly fishing, especially for trout, is a popular activity in New Zealand. This style of fishing is an art form as much as a sport, requiring precision, patience, and knowledge of the natural environment.

Standing thigh-deep in a clear, rushing river surrounded by New Zealand's magnificent surroundings is an experience in and of itself. Add the exhilaration of casting the right fly and tempting a trout to bite, and you have a fishing adventure to remember.

Tips and Techniques

Fly fishing is a skill that requires practice. It entails learning how to effectively cast the fly line, knowing which sort of fly to use depending on the conditions and comprehending trout behavior and habitat.

Thoughts

Some rivers in New Zealand are only for fly fishing, and many require catch-and-release to protect the trout population. Always double-check local restrictions before venturing out.

Kayak Fishing Adventure

Kayak fishing is a terrific choice for anyone searching for a more immersive and energetic fishing experience. This strategy allows you to get closer to the action and explore locations that larger boats cannot.

The Experience

Paddling a kayak through the calm waters of a bay or down a scenic river provides a sense of peace and connection with nature. Because of the quietness and flexibility of a kayak, you can often approach fish without frightening them, leading to some wonderful fishing opportunities.

Tips and Techniques

When kayak fishing, balance, and silence are essential. Any rapid movements can flip the kayak over or scare the fish away. It's also important to think about safety, such as using a personal flotation device and avoiding going too far offshore, especially if you're new to kayak fishing.

Considerations

Before going kayak fishing, always check the weather forecast. Wind, waves, and currents can all have a big impact on your safety and success.

In New Zealand, going fishing is more than simply a pastime—it's a way to interact with the country's breathtaking landscape and revel in the many ways the catch can be enjoyed. Every angler may find their own particular adventure in New Zealand's various waters, whether it's battling a huge game fish in the deep sea, matching wits with a tricky trout on a fly, or discreetly gliding in a kayak into a potential fishing site. Remember that the journey is just as important as the catch, and every fishing excursion is a chance to create memorable memories.

The Best Time to Fish in New Zealand

The two main islands of New Zealand offer a variety of fishing opportunities for both novice and experienced anglers. The variety of fish species and the diversity of the waters make it a popular destination for fishing aficionados from all over the world.

Seasonal Fishing Calendars

Summer (December to February)

Summer is an excellent season for fishing in New Zealand.

Freshwater and saltwater fishing are both at their best. In the coastal waters, you can expect to see a variety of species, such as snapper, kingfish, and kahawai. Trout and salmon can be caught in freshwater.

Autumn (March to May)

This is an excellent period for trout fishing, especially in South Island rivers.

Winter (June-August)

While many fish are less active during the winter, certain forms of fishing can still be successful. It's a terrific time to capture rainbow trout in the North Island's Lake Taupo, for example, because this is their spawning season.

Spring (September to November)

Spring heralds the start of whitebait season on the West Coast, a New Zealand delicacy. During this time, sea-run trout begin to migrate, making it perfect for river and estuary fishing.

The Effect of Weather on Fishing

The weather has a big impact on fishing in New Zealand. In fact, it can be the deciding factor in whether or not you go fishing on a given day.

Temperature

Because fish are cold-blooded, water temperature might alter their activity levels. When the weather warms up, fish become more active and more inclined to bite. This is one of the reasons that summer is such a popular fishing season. During the summer, however, water temperatures might become too warm for certain species, such as trout, making early morning and late evening the optimal times to fish.

Rain

Rain has a variety of effects on fishing. Heavy rain can cause rivers to swell and discolor, making fishing difficult. Light rain, on the other hand, can be advantageous, especially for trout fishing, because it can stir up insects and other food sources, encouraging fish to feed.

Wind

Wind can have an effect on the sea's conditions as well as the visibility of your bait. A little to moderate breeze, in general, might be advantageous for sea fishing since it stirs up the water and makes fish less cautious. Strong winds, on the other hand, can make fishing unsafe, especially for small boats or shore fishing.

Remember that safety should always come first when fishing. Before venturing out, always verify the local weather and sea conditions, and make sure you have the necessary safety equipment.

The Role of a Professional Outfitter in New Zealand Fishing

Fishing in New Zealand is an exciting and gratifying hobby, but tourists may find it difficult to negotiate the strange terrain and rules. This is when a professional outfitter's knowledge comes in handy. Here's an explanation of what role a professional outfitter plays in ensuring the success of your fishing trip in New Zealand.

Professional Advice and Instruction

A professional outfitter can provide specialized assistance and instruction to enhance your fishing experience, whether you're a seasoned angler or new to the sport. They can teach proper tactics, recommend the most successful baits and lures, and assist you with improving your casting or reeling-in abilities.

Their skills can be especially useful for specific fishing techniques, such as fly fishing. They can teach you everything from casting techniques to fly selection and knowing local trout behavior.

Understanding of Local Fishing Spots

One of the most significant benefits of working with a professional outfitter is their deep knowledge of local fishing areas. They know the best sites to capture various species at different seasons of the year and can lead you to off-the-beaten-path locations, enhancing your chances of a successful catch.

Understanding Conservation Regulations and Practices

Fishing legislation in New Zealand can be complicated, with distinct rules governing different regions, species, and techniques of fishing. A professional outfitter is familiar with these restrictions and can verify that you are fishing legally and ethically.

Outfitters are also important conservationists. They teach anglers about the necessity of catch-and-release, correct fish handling, and adhering to bag and size limitations, all of which contribute to the sustainability of New Zealand's fishing resources.

Provision and Maintenance of Equipment

Professional outfitters provide high-quality fishing equipment that is specifically customized to the type of fishing you will be performing. This means you don't have to bring or buy your own equipment, which is very convenient for international guests. They guarantee that all equipment is kept in good condition and is appropriate for the local environment and targeted species.

Security

When fishing, safety is of the utmost importance, especially in unfamiliar or difficult areas. Outfitters are trained in safety measures and first aid, and they make certain that all safety laws are observed. They are aware of local weather trends and potential threats, and they have emergency preparedness strategies in place.

Hiring a skilled outfitter can improve your fishing experience in New Zealand greatly. Their skill, local knowledge, and assistance can not only assist you in catching fish but also in doing it safely, ethically, and in a manner that respects the local ecology and adds to the long-term viability of this valued sport. Whether you're looking for a certain species, want to try a new fishing method, or simply want to have a great fishing expedition, hiring a skilled outfitter is an investment that will pay off in wonderful memories.

This chapter has covered a wide range of topics related to fishing in New Zealand, from understanding seasonal fishing calendars to the impact of weather on fishing activities. We've looked at the differences between saltwater and freshwater fishing, the best species to target at different times of the year, and how weather, rain, and Wind affect fishing conditions. We've also discussed the rules and regulations that govern fishing in New Zealand. These restrictions are in place to protect both anglers and the country's unique marine and freshwater environments. Understanding and following these principles not only ensures a sustainable fishing environment but also contributes to a more rewarding and trouble-free fishing experience.

While understanding these criteria is essential for good fishing, nothing beats the knowledge of a competent outfitter. They have the necessary local knowledge, equipment, and safety training to navigate New Zealand's varied fishing landscapes. A professional outfitter can direct you to the best fishing places, teach you the skills required for different species, and assist you with weather forecasting and safety precautions. Hiring a competent outfitter can, therefore, substantially improve your fishing experience in New Zealand, transforming a decent trip into an outstanding one.

Chapter 13
What's the Catch?

In the previous chapter, we looked at the best places on the South and the North Islands for fishing, learned about fishing licenses and regulations, and explored different fishing methods like deep-sea charter, fly fishing, and kayak fishing.

In this chapter, we will dive through the mesmerizing waterways of this island nation, revealing the diverse fish species that live there as well as the exciting experiences that wait beneath the water's surface. This chapter will discuss each fish species in detail and learn about the best seasons and tips and tricks to hunt them.

New Zealand, surrounded by the wide Pacific Ocean and dotted with various lakes and rivers, has a plethora of fishing opportunities. From the North Island's glittering turquoise waters to the South Island's deep, calm lakes, each place has its own attraction, offering an angler's paradise set among stunning landscapes.

Seawater Fishing

The seawaters of New Zealand are teeming with a diverse range of fish species. These waters are well-known for big-game fishing and provide the exhilarating excitement of catching Billfish and Marlins. Slower but equally rewarding encounters await with species such as Tuna, Kingfish, and the popular Snappers, each of which has its own set of challenges and rewards for the discerning angler.

Freshwater Fishing

Moving inland, the freshwater ecosystems of New Zealand are equally rewarding. New Zealand's pristine lakes and rivers, known for their crystal-clear waters, provide world-class Trout and salmon fishing. These secretive and combative species make freshwater fishing an exercise in skill and patience.

Conservation and Sustainability

Aside from the pleasure of the catch, New Zealand's fishing sector is intertwined with conservation and sustainable methods. Understanding and following local rules, like bag limits and size limits, is critical to maintaining these unique habitats for future generations of anglers.

We will go into these issues in depth in this chapter, providing essential insights into each fish species, excellent fishing spots, effective fishing tactics, and key legislation to guide your New Zealand fishing journey. Let us set out on this adventure together, investigating the mysteries of the deep and unveiling the catch that could be at the end of your line.

New Zealand Seawater Fishing

New Zealand's 15,000-kilometer-long coastline provides some of the world's best seawater fishing opportunities. With a diverse range of species inhabiting its maritime waters, New Zealand is a dream destination for both big game and leisure fishermen.

Billfish: The Giants of the Ocean

The beautiful billfish, true ocean giants, are one of the most sought-after catches in New Zealand's waters. They have an exceptional combination of size, speed, and strength, making them a worthy adversary for even the most seasoned fisherman.

Common Billfish Species in New Zealand

Billfish species found in New Zealand seas include the Striped Marlin, Blue Marlin, and Broadbill Swordfish. These massive fish are best known for their elongated bills, known as rostrums, which they employ to stun their victims.

Best Bill-fishing Seasons and Locations

Billfish season normally lasts from December to April. The warm waters of the North Island, particularly the Bay of Islands and the Northland region, are among the best places to catch billfish. Another popular area is the famed King Bank, which is noted for producing large catches.

Recommendations for Gear and Techniques

Robust fishing gear is required when pursuing billfish. Big-game reels with a capacity of 600-1000 yards of line, along with strong rods, are advised. Use different trolling lures or live bait, such as skipjack tuna. It's critical to understand that capturing billfish is a collaborative endeavor that frequently involves a skillful boat handler and an angler with a fighting chair.

Catching a billfish in New Zealand's waters is a feat that represents the peak of an angler's career. When hooked, these giants put up an amazing struggle, making them one of the most exciting fish to catch. But keep in mind that patience, planning, and respect for these amazing creatures are essential in this pursuit. Prepare to find even more amazing creatures that await your bait and hook as we go deeper into the world of New Zealand's Ocean fishing.

Marlins: The Speedsters

Marlins are undoubtedly the most recognizable game fish, known for their incredible speed and airborne acrobatics when hooked. Their long, slender bodies and sharply pointed bills distinguish them, and their aggressive eating habits give anglers an intriguing challenge.

Common Marlin Species in New Zealand

Blue marlin, striped marlin, and the rare Black marlin are the most common marlin species found in New Zealand seas. The most frequent of these is the Striped Marlin, which is famed for its vivid, vertical blue stripes that light up during a battle. Although less common, the Blue Marlin is regarded for its tremendous size, with some captures topping 900 pounds.

Best Marlin Catching Times and Locations

Marlin season in New Zealand normally runs from January to April, coinciding with the warmest water temperatures. The upper North Island offers the best marlin fishing prospects. The Bay of Islands, the Northland coast, and offshore banks like the Mokohinau Islands and the Three Kings Islands are popular destinations.

Recommendations for Gear and Techniques

Because of the strength and speed of these fish, marlin fishing requires tough and dependable equipment. Heavy-duty trolling reels with at least 500 yards of 80 to 130-pound test line and a strong 5.5 to the 7-foot rod are typically recommended. Rigged trolling lures or live baits like skipjack or yellowfin tuna are frequently employed.

When fighting a marlin, expert boat handling is essential. To keep up with the fast-swimming fish, the fisherman frequently reverses the boat while maintaining consistent pressure. It's also critical to be ready for a possibly lengthy encounter, as marlins are known to fight tenaciously.

Getting a marlin is, without a doubt, one of the most exciting moments in sport fishing. These speedsters' explosive strikes, powerful runs, and aerial displays create a challenge that requires skill, strength, and stamina. Remember that the thrill of the pursuit is just as satisfying as the catch itself when you set out in search of these majestic creatures. Next, we'll explore the realm of another high-energy foe, the Tuna.

Tuna: The Endurance Athletes

One cannot discuss seawater fishing without mentioning the magnificent Tuna. Tuna are the ocean's endurance athletes, distinguished by their bullet-shaped bodies, metallic coloring, and incredible swimming speed. Their rapid, long-distance swimming and battling spirit make them a popular target for fishermen all around the world.

Tunas. Native to New Zealand

The most prevalent tuna species found in New Zealand waters are yellowfin, albacore, and bluefin tuna. Yellowfin Tuna are renowned for their exquisite meat, whereas Albacore Tuna while being smaller, are plentiful and popular for trolling.

The Best Times and Places to Catch Tuna

Tuna fishing in New Zealand normally peaks between January and April, with Albacore Tuna accessible as early as

November. The Bay of Plenty, Northland, and offshore banks such as the Three Kings Islands and the Ranfurly Banks are all prominent sites.

Gear Suggestions and Techniques

Tuna fishing demands heavy equipment. It is recommended to use heavy-duty spinning or trolling gear capable of holding 300-500 yards of 50–80-pound test line. Skirted trolling lures, cedar plugs, and live baits such as mackerel are common.

Trolling at higher speeds than other species is frequently used in this strategy. Anglers should be prepared for long, tough struggles once hooked, as Tuna are famed for their stamina and strength.

Kingfish: The Fighters

The Kingfish of New Zealand, also known as Yellowtail Kingfish or Haku, are famous for their persistent fighting and strong runs. They are easily identified by their striking yellow tail, dark green body, and visible lateral line.

Kingfish Species Common to New Zealand

The Yellowtail Kingfish is the most common species in New Zealand. Kingfish is a huge, strong fish that can reach weights of up to 50kg (110 lbs.), though most captured are between 10-15 kg (22-33 lbs.).

The Best Times and Places to Catch Kingfish

Kingfish can be caught all year in New Zealand; however, the peak season is usually between December and April. The Bay of Islands, Coromandel Peninsula, and Hauraki Gulf are all notable sites.

Gear Suggestions and Techniques

To handle these huge fish, you'll need a strong, solid tackle. Medium to heavy rods are commonly used, along with high-capacity spinning or conventional reels spooled with 30–50-pound test lines. Live baits such as piper, squid, or mackerel, as well as lures such as poppers, stick baits, and jigs, are frequently utilized.

Because of their first powerful runs and penchant for rushing into rocky obstacles to get loose, kingfish require careful handling and strength to land.

Whether you're up against Tuna's enormous endurance or a Kingfish's explosive power, saltwater fishing in New Zealand offers intriguing challenges for every angler. As you go on these aquatic adventures, keep in mind that each species presents a unique experience that necessitates various talents and methods.

Snappers: The Popular Targets

Snapper fishing has a particular place in the hearts of both natives and visitors in New Zealand. Snappers are among the most popularly sought species, prized for their delicious eating characteristics and exciting combat. Whether you're a seasoned angler or a newbie, these crimson-scaled monsters provide a rewarding fishing experience.

Common Snapper Species in New Zealand

The principal species found in New Zealand seas is Pagrus auratus, sometimes known as Snapper. Snapper can be distinguished by their pink to scarlet coloration, sloping forehead, and a pronounced hump near the skull.

The Best Times and Places to Catch Snappers

Snapper can be taken all year, but the best time to catch them is from October to April when they migrate into shallower waters to spawn. On the North Island, prime Snapper fishing spots include the Hauraki Gulf, Bay of Islands, and Bay of Plenty. Snappers are abundant in the Marlborough Sounds and Golden Bay on the South Island.

Gear Suggestions and Techniques

Depending on the approach employed, snapper fishing requires a variety of equipment. Light to medium weight spinning or overhead gear is typical, and a 10-20lb line is usually adequate. Snapper aren't picky when it comes to bait, and their preferences include squid, pilchards, and shellfish.

The popular technique to catch Snapper is Stray lining, in which the bait is allowed to 'stray' down through the water column. Soft baiting and gentle jigging have also grown in favor in recent years as a means of luring Snapper.

The thrill of catching a Snapper in New Zealand's seas brings fishermen returning time and time again. Snapper is a popular target because of their widespread existence, aggressive feeding behavior, and the wonderful reward they provide.

Freshwater Fishing in New Zealand

Aside from the salty ocean waves, New Zealand also has some of the best freshwater fishing in the world. Its serene lakes and pure rivers, many of which are tucked within breathtaking scenery, and teeming with an abundance of fish species, making it a must-see for any avid freshwater angler.

Trout: The Delicate Challenge

Trout fishing is a popular sport in New Zealand. The challenge of hooking these elusive fish and the skill necessary to pull them in has attracted anglers all over the world.

Common Trout Species in New Zealand

The Rainbow and Brown Trout are the two most common trout species in New Zealand. Brown Trout are prized for their cleverness, which makes them more difficult to capture, but

Rainbow Trout are noted for their acrobatics and furious struggle when hooked.

Best Times and Places to Catch Trout

While Trout can be caught all year, the best time to catch them is from October to April. The Taupo region, the Tongariro River, and the Nelson and Canterbury districts of the South Island are all excellent trout fishing destinations.

Recommendations for Gear and Techniques

For trout fishing, lightweight rods (between 6 and 7 feet long) with a spinning reel and 4–8-pound line are typically employed. Flies, spinners, and spoons are popular bait choices.

Fly fishing is especially popular in New Zealand, with the most frequent tactics being nymphing and dry fly. Because Trout are known for their wariness and selective feeding habits, patience and precision are essential.

Salmon: The River Runners

If catching Trout in New Zealand's freshwater poses a delicate challenge, then catching Salmon, who are known for their speed, represents the opposite. Catching a Salmon, known for its epic migrations and strong fights, is a highlight for many fishermen.

Common Salmon Species in New Zealand

The Chinook, commonly known as the King Salmon, is the most common type of Salmon found in New Zealand. They are the largest Pacific Salmon species and are prized for their size, strength, and culinary value.

Best Times and Places to Catch Salmon

Salmon fishing in New Zealand is best from December to March when the Salmon are spawning up the rivers. South Island hotspots include the Rakaia, Waimakariri, and Waitaki Rivers.

Recommendations for Gear and Techniques

Because of the size and power of these fish, salmon fishing demands heavy-duty gear. Medium to heavy rods are advised, along with a strong spinning reel and 15-20lb line. Spinners, spoons, and salmon eggs are popular baits.

Casting and trolling are popular methods. Salmon are famed for their strength and durability, so be prepared for a fierce fight once hooked.

Freshwater fishing in New Zealand offers a varied and diverse experience that is sure to satisfy every angler, from the elusive Trout to the gigantic Salmon. Remember that each cast is a new experience ready to emerge as you immerse yourself in the tranquil beauty of these watery habitats. As time goes on, we'll take a deeper look at the legislation that will ensure these spectacular fishing experiences are preserved for future generations.

Knowing the Rules and Regulations

Before casting a line into New Zealand's bountiful waters, it's critical to become acquainted with the local fishing rules and regulations. These standards are in place not only to safeguard the varied species that live within these habitats but also to ensure that everyone has an equitable fishing experience. Understanding and complying with these restrictions as an overseas tourist is part of your trip into New Zealand's unique angling culture. We will present a full explanation of bag limits, size restrictions, and specific laws for both ocean and freshwater species in this section, preparing you for a safe and rewarding fishing excursion.

An Overview of New Zealand Fishing Regulations

It is important to follow fishing rules and regulations if we want fishing resources to last. Rules and regulations contribute to the protection and maintenance of fish stocks, ensuring that future generations can enjoy the exhilarating experience of fishing in New Zealand. This section provides an overview of the key rules and regulations that you should be aware of as an international tourist before embarking on your fishing experience.

The Importance of Following Local Rules and Regulations

Following local rules and regulations strictly is not only a legal necessity but also an ethical obligation to the environment. It's all about respecting the law, nature, and future generations of fishermen. Breaching these restrictions can result in serious penalties, such as substantial fines and equipment confiscation. Furthermore, compliance ensures the survival of various species, which contributes to a healthy and functioning ecosystem.

Overview of Bag Restrictions and Size Limits

Bag limitations and size restrictions are in place to prevent overfishing and allow fish to mature and spawn. Size constraints provide the minimum (and occasionally maximum) length of fish that can be maintained, whereas bag limits specify the maximum number of fish that a fisherman can keep in one day. These limits and restrictions differ depending on the species and locality, so it's critical to double-check the exact guidelines for your fishing site.

Specific Guidelines for Freshwater and Seawater Species

Each fish species, whether in saltwater or freshwater, has its own set of laws. In most regions, the bag restriction for Snapper is seven per person per day, with a minimum size limit of 30 cm. In contrast, freshwater fishing restrictions vary greatly depending on the area. A maximum of six Trout can be taken per day in some places. It should be noted that in some trophy trout areas, catch-and-release is required. The laws for Salmon vary depending on the season and the river system.

Understanding the Requirement for a Fishing License

To fish in New Zealand as an international visitor, you'll need a license for both saltwater and freshwater fishing. Freshwater fishing licenses are especially stringent, with different localities requiring distinct licenses.

In New Zealand, fishing isn't possible without knowing and following the local rules and laws. As an overseas visitor or tourist, your cooperation ensures the viability and survival of New Zealand's diverse fish species. By knowing and following these rules, you help make New Zealand one of the best places to fish in the world.

New Zealand Conservation Efforts

As we embark on the thrilling voyage of fishing in New Zealand's seas, we must recognize the arduous work that goes into maintaining and protecting these valuable ecosystems. The country's beautiful landscapes and diverse wildlife are a result of considerable conservation efforts over the years.

In this section, we'll look at the importance of sustainable fishing techniques, the vital contributions of local conservation organizations, and how you, as an international tourist, can help maintain New Zealand's various aquatic habitats.

The Value of Sustainable Fishing Methods

Sustainable fishing techniques are critical to the health of New Zealand's aquatic ecosystems. Overfishing, habitat degradation, and pollution can quickly upset the delicate balance of these ecosystems. Anglers may help conserve these dynamic aquatic ecosystems and their various species by complying with bag limits, size limitations, and other rules.

Local Conservation Organizations' Role

Many local conservation groups work tirelessly to maintain and improve New Zealand's fishing resources. These groups undertake research, advocate for sustainable fishing practices, and work on habitat restoration initiatives. Angler rights are advocated for by organizations such as the New Zealand Sport Fishing Council and Fish & Game New Zealand, which also promote conservation and sustainability.

What Tourists and International Visitors Can Do

Tourists and international visitors can help to preserve New Zealand's vibrant aquatic habitats. You may have a wonderful fishing experience while reducing your environmental impact by following regulations, practicing catch and release, and respecting protected areas.

Participating in local conservation programs, such as clean-up days or habitat restoration projects, can also provide a deeper connection to the environment. Purchasing fishing licenses and permits also contributes to conservation efforts, as the monies are frequently used to support fish population management and enhancement.

Remember that each fishing excursion is about more than simply the catch; it's about enjoying the voyage, learning from the experience, and engaging with nature in a responsible manner. Familiarize yourself with the restrictions of your chosen fishing spot, keep the ecology in mind, and don't be hesitant to seek help from local fishermen or conservation agents.

All in all, fishing in New Zealand is a privilege that comes with obligations. Respect the environment, follow the rules, and help the ongoing efforts to preserve these magnificent fishing possibilities for future generations.

Chapter 14
Hunting and Fishing

As we reach the end of this book, we urge you to explore the fascinating world of hunting and fishing in New Zealand. We have methodically examined the delights of this gorgeous country in the preceding pages, immersing ourselves in its colorful culture, awe-inspiring scenery, and incredible animals.

In this chapter, we will discuss a thorough compilation of the knowledge and insights obtained, focusing on the subtle intricacies of hunting and fishing in New Zealand. Within these pages, you will find a wealth of material that has been thoughtfully prepared to provide a thorough understanding of these beloved outdoor sports.

This chapter serves as a definitive guide to the exceptional experiences that await you, whether you are an adventurous adventurer looking for the thrill of the chase or a fisherman looking for undisturbed fishing grounds.

In our endeavor to illustrate the significance, benefits, and attractiveness of hunting and fishing in New Zealand, we have left no stone unturned. The tapestry of delights awaits those who wish to indulge in New Zealand's ancient traditions of hunting and fishing.

The Attraction of New Zealand's Hunting and Fishing

Hunting and fishing are undeniably attractive sports in New Zealand. This island nation entices outdoor enthusiasts with its abundance of natural beauty and promises unrivaled hunting and fishing experiences.

Pristine Natural Setting

The untouched splendor of New Zealand's environment is simply breathtaking. Majestic mountains, lush woods, crystal-clear lakes, and pure rivers provide an idyllic setting for hunting and fishing activities. The country's distinctive flora and fauna add to its allure, displaying incredible ecological diversity and setting the stage for unforgettable adventures in the great outdoors.

Rich Sporting Tradition

Hunting and fishing are strongly ingrained in New Zealand's culture and are an important element of the country's rich recreational legacy. These activities passed down through generations, have importance beyond simply leisure. They represent a connection to the land, a reverence for wildlife, and a celebration of the country's history and identity. In order to truly enjoy the experience, visitors can immerse themselves in New Zealand's vibrant sporting culture through hunting and fishing.

Wide Range of Game and Fish Species

New Zealand has a vast range of game animals and fish species, making it a hunting and fishing paradise. The land offers a broad assortment of game animals for hunters, from stately red deer to agile chamois, elusive tahr to wild boar. Meanwhile, rivers, lakes, and coastal waters are teeming with a variety of fish, including the classic trout, salmon, snapper, and even the huge marlin. The plethora of game and fish species guarantees that hunters andanglers will have plenty of opportunities to put their skills and knowledge to the test.

Exotic Hunting and Fishing Adventures

Hunting and fishing in New Zealand are absolutely unique experiences. The rough countryside beckons hunters to embark on difficult treks in search of prize animals in their native habitats. The thrill of the pursuit, the stunning scenery, and the joy of a successful hunt all leave lasting impressions. Casting lines in New Zealand's gorgeous fishing sites is an equally enthralling experience for anglers. Fishing in New Zealand is an amazing sport, whether wading in a lonely river or trekking into the enormous ocean. The sense of adventure, connection with nature, and the possibility of an extraordinary catch make it an exhilarating pastime.

Joshua Godfrey

Explore the Advantages of Hunting in New Zealand

Wildlife Balance Preservation

Hunting is critical to maintaining New Zealand's delicate wildlife balance. It helps to manage populations and maintain native species as a vital part of conservation efforts. Understanding the significance of hunting from this perspective allows us to grasp how it contributes to the country's overall ecological health.

The value of hunting in conservation efforts: Hunting is an important tool in wildlife management tactics aimed at protecting the ecological balance of New Zealand's ecosystems. Authorities can control and preserve game animal populations through properly regulated hunting programs, minimizing overgrazing and habitat destruction. Hunting helps to guarantee the availability of appropriate resources for both wildlife and natural plants by regulating population levels.

Population Management and Native Species Protection

Invasive species represent substantial dangers to New Zealand's unique biodiversity. Hunting is critical in managing and controlling invasive animals that compete with or prey on native fauna. Hunters help to defend and preserve native species by deliberately hunting invasive animals. This intervention helps to maintain ecological integrity by allowing native plants and animals to thrive in the absence of invasive predators or rivals.

208

Hunting and Fishing in New Zealand

Hunting in New Zealand provides tremendous benefits for wildlife conservation and the protection of local species. Hunters who participate in regulated hunting programs actively contribute to the management of game animal populations, the prevention of habitat damage, and the overall health of the ecosystem. Furthermore, by targeting exotic species, hunters help to safeguard New Zealand's native flora and animals. We can maintain the delicate balance of wildlife by responsible hunting techniques, ensuring the long-term sustainability of the country's natural ecosystems.

Increasing Biodiversity and Ecosystem Health

Introduction: Hunting in New Zealand not only helps with animal management, but it also helps to improve biodiversity and maintain healthy environments. We can grasp how these behaviors enhance the general health of the country's ecosystems by knowing the favorable influence of hunting on ecological variety and the relevance of selective culling.

Positive Impact on Ecological Diversity

Hunting, when done ethically and with an emphasis on sustainability, has the potential to increase ecological diversity in New Zealand. Hunters help to minimize overpopulation and reduce competition for resources by selectively removing particular species. As a result, other species can thrive, increasing overall biodiversity. Hunting promotes the coexistence of many species by carefully regulating populations, resulting in a healthier and more resilient ecosystem.

Maintaining Healthy Habitats Through Selected Culling

An important part of responsible hunting is selective culling, which plays a critical role in maintaining healthy ecosystems. Hunters can remove individuals that may be harmful to the ecosystem by targeting specific individuals within a community. In locations where overgrazing occurs, for example, deliberately hunting herbivorous species can help manage their numbers and minimize vegetation damage. This proactive strategy keeps environments balanced, allowing local flora and fauna to thrive.

Hunting in New Zealand not only helps with wildlife management but it also boosts biodiversity and preserves healthy environments. Hunters contribute to the overall health and diversity of the country's ecosystems through responsible hunting techniques and selective culling. Hunting contributes to the creation of balanced environments in which multiple species can coexist by preventing overcrowding and controlling species interactions. These initiatives are critical in preserving New Zealand's natural history and ensuring the survival of its distinctive flora and animals.

Economic Contributions

Hunting is important not just for the environment but also

for the economy in New Zealand. The hunting business is critical in terms of supporting local economies, producing job opportunities, and generating cash. By investigating the economic benefits of hunting, we may realize its significance beyond conservation and leisure.

Hunting Industry's Contributions to the Local Economy

The hunting industry in New Zealand has a considerable impact on the local economy. Visitors from all over the world are drawn to the country's exceptional hunting prospects, fueling tourism and related economic activities. Outfitters, lodges, guides, and other businesses cater to hunters' requirements by offering services and lodgings that benefit the industry. The revenue created by hunting-related activities helps to expand and develop local communities, promoting economic stability and prosperity.

Job Creation and Revenue Generation

Hunting generates employment opportunities in a variety of industries. The sector employs a wide spectrum of people, from guides and outfitters to hospitality workers and transportation providers. Local communities benefit from these job opportunities, which not only help individuals and their families but also contribute to the region's general economic development. Furthermore, hunting-related expenditures such as licenses, permits, equipment purchases, and lodging produce cash that feeds into local companies and government agencies, encouraging economic growth even further.

Hunting is an important economic activity in New Zealand, contributing to the local economy through job creation and revenue generation. The hunting industry supports a wide range of enterprises and job sectors, creating opportunities for individuals while also supporting local communities.

The capital spent on hunting activities helps local companies, promoting economic growth and prosperity. Recognizing hunting's economic contributions emphasizes its varied significance, framing it as an activity that not only supports conservation efforts and recreational pursuits but also plays an important part in supporting livelihoods and community well-being.

Exploring the Benefits of Fishing New Zealand

The waterways of New Zealand are brimming with an astounding variety of fish species, providing anglers with unrivaled chances and benefits. The different aquatic habitats of the country, which include rivers, lakes, and coastal areas, provide a fertile base for abundant fish populations and unique fishing experiences.

The sheer number of fish species accessible is a key advantage of fishing in New Zealand. Anglers can target trout, salmon, snapper, marlin, and other species. This range appeals to all preferences and skill levels, providing an interesting and gratifying fishing adventure for anglers of all ages.

Abundance of Fish Species

Fishing in New Zealand has numerous advantages, beginning with the number of fish species found in its waterways. The great marine biodiversity of the country provides fishermen with unrivaled opportunities for different fishing experiences. We can appreciate the particular benefits of fishing in New Zealand by recognizing the significance of this abundance and the variety of fishing experiences offered.

The Abundant Marine Biodiversity in New Zealand's Waters

The waters of New Zealand are home to a diverse range of fish species. The country's marine biodiversity is breathtaking, from its clean rivers and lakes to its huge coastline areas. Anglers can pursue species such as trout, salmon, snapper, kahawai, kingfish, and even marlin. The variety of fish species demonstrates the health and vigor of New Zealand's marine ecosystems, providingfishermen with a plethora of options and possibilities to seek their desired catch.

Opportunities for a Variety of Fishing Experiences

New Zealand fishing offers to anglers of all interests and ability levels. Whether you prefer to fly fishing in clean streams, casting from the beaches of beautiful lakes, or go out to the open ocean for big-game fishing, the country has it all. Each fishing expedition has its own set of difficulties and rewards, providing a tapestry of possibilities that appeal to fishermen looking for new experiences. New Zealand's numerous fishing experiences ensure that there is something for everyone, from quiet locations to exhilarating offshore adventures.

The plethora of fish species found in New Zealand's waterways, as well as the variety of fishing experiences available, enhance the benefits of fishing there. The abundant marine variety demonstrates the health and vigor of the country's ecosystems, providing anglers with a diverse range of fish species to pursue. New Zealand caters to a wide range of fishing interests and skill levels, from quiet freshwater fishing to adventurous offshore expeditions. Anglers looking for a quiet angling experience or a dramatic encounter with a monster fish will find it in the seas of New Zealand.

Sustainable Fishing Methods

New Zealand fishing is distinguished not just by the abundance of fish species but also by a strong dedication to sustainable fishing practices. To safeguard fish supplies and maintain the long-term viability of its fisheries, the government has established conservation measures and laws. Understanding the significance of sustainable fishing practices allows us to comprehend how New Zealand works to protect its fish species for future generations.

Conservation Measures and Regulations

To properly manage its fisheries, New Zealand has adopted a comprehensive framework of conservation measures and laws. Size and bag limits, seasonal restrictions, and fishing quotas are examples of these policies. The government intends to combat overfishing and encourage sustainable fishing practices by setting limitations on fishing activity. These laws are intended to achieve a balance between recreational and commercial fishing while also safeguarding the health of fish populations and their ecosystems.

Protecting Stocks for Future Generations

New Zealand's commitment to sustainable fishing techniques reflects a long-term vision of protecting fish stocks for future generations. The country ensures that fish populations may replenish and grow by enacting measures to minimize fishing pressure and promote responsible harvesting. This emphasis on sustainable methods helps to preserve the delicate balance of marine ecosystems, protecting not only the fish but also the larger biodiversity that is dependent on healthy fish populations.

Sustainable fishing methods are at the heart of New Zealand's fishing industry, driven by the country's commitment to safeguarding fish stocks and guaranteeing the long-term viability of its fisheries. Sustainable measures and regulations show a proactive approach to managing fishing operations and conserving the integrity of marine ecosystems. By implementing sustainable techniques, New Zealand protects its fish populations, guaranteeing that future generations can continue to enjoy the country's bountiful fishing resources. Anglers contribute to the preservation of fish supplies and play an active role in preserving the natural balance of New Zealand's waters through appropriate fishing methods.

Recreation and Well-Being

Fishing in New Zealand not only provides opportunities for catching fish but it also provides several recreational and health benefits. Fishing as a recreational sport helps to relieve stress, and the health benefits and therapeutic features of the experience add to general well-being. Understanding the enjoyment and health benefits of fishing allows us to appreciate the overall benefits it provides to individuals.

Fishing as a Recreational Activity and Stress-Reliever

Fishing is often viewed as a pleasurable, relaxing, and exciting recreational activity. The tranquil ambiance of tranquil lakes, rivers, or coastal places gives a peaceful retreat from the rigors of daily life. Casting a line, waiting patiently, and interacting with nature all contribute to a peaceful and immersive experience. Fishing's repetitive action and attention can have a relaxing effect, decreasing tension and increasing mental well-being. Fishing, whether alone or with family and friends, provides great possibilities for bonding, making lasting memories, and seeking peace in nature.

Health Benefits and Therapeutic Aspects of Fishing

Spending time outside and engaging in physical exercises, such as casting and pulling in fish, improves fitness and stamina. Walking, wading, or boat handling are common activities associated with fishing, giving possibilities for exercise and cardiovascular health. Furthermore, exposure to sunlight when fishing assists the body in absorbing critical vitamin D, which is important for bone health and overall well-being. Catching a fish provides a sense of accomplishment and satisfaction that can increase self-esteem and foster a happy mental state.

Fishing in New Zealand is more than just a pleasant pastime; it also has health benefits. It relieves stress by providing a calm respite and an opportunity to interact with nature. Fishing has many health benefits, including physical activity, exposure to sunlight, and a sense of accomplishment. Fishing helps people unwind, recharge, and find joy in the tranquil beauty of New Zealand's seas. Fishing in New Zealand is a gratifying and revitalizing experience for both body and mind, whether you are looking for leisure, adventure, or a therapeutic retreat.

Importance of Hiring Outfitters for Hunting and Fishing

Hiring expert and experienced outfitter for hunting and fishing in New Zealand is critical for a number of reasons. The outfitter brings a wealth of knowledge, experience, and resources to the table, assuring a successful and thrilling excursion. Here are some of the most important reasons for employing a professional outfitter:

Local Knowledge and Expertise

Professional outfitters are well-versed in the local geography, wildlife behavior, fishing locations, and hunting rules. Their knowledge is based on years of exploring New Zealand's different landscapes and learning the nuances of hunting and fishing in certain places. They can provide useful information on the finest hunting and fishing techniques, great locations, and the best times to pursue various species. Using their knowledge raises the likelihood of a profitable and rewarding experience.

Legal Compliance and Safety

Hunting and fishing in New Zealand are subject to strict safety measures and legal requirements. Professional outfitters guarantee that all activities are carried out in a safe and responsible manner, putting their clients' safety first. They understand the local rules and regulations concerning licensing, permits, bag limits, and catch-and-release methods. Hunters and fishermen can have peace of mind knowing that they are operating within the legal framework and minimizing any hazards associated with the activities by employing experienced outfitters.

Exclusive Access to Locations and Resources

Professional outfitters frequently have access to unique hunting and fishing locations that the general public may not have. These areas are carefully surveyed and chosen based on their potential for effective hunting and fishing. Furthermore, outfitters may have partnerships or agreements with landowners or private reserves that allow their clients' exclusive access to outstanding hunting and fishing regions. By hiring professional outfitters, tourists can explore hidden gems and maximize their chances of encountering trophy games or abundant fish populations.

Tools and Equipment

Outfitters often supply high-quality equipment and gear for hunting and fishing trips. They make certain that consumers have the necessary tools, such as weapons, fishing rods, reels, tackle, and safety equipment. Professional outfitters also maintain and upgrade their equipment on a regular basis to ensure peak performance and dependability. This eliminates the need for individuals to invest in specific equipment, particularly for those traveling from abroad. By depending on outfitters for equipment, hunters, and anglers may concentrate on the experience rather than the hassle of collecting and transporting specialized equipment.

Individualized Experiences and Support

Professional outfitters provide individualized and bespoke experiences depending on the interests, skill levels, and desired goals of their clients. They recognize that each hunter or fisherman has different goals and needs, and they work hard to meet those expectations. Throughout the hunting or fishing expedition, outfitters provide advice, assistance, and teaching, as well as useful insights and ideas to maximize success. Their knowledge and tailored approach ensure that clients have a memorable and rewarding experience, whether it is their first-time hunting or fishing in New Zealand or they are seasoned lovers.

Subsequently, employing experienced outfitters for hunting and fishing in New Zealand is critical for improving the whole experience. Their local knowledge, safety precautions, access to rare areas, quality equipment, and personalized support assure a successful, pleasurable, and well-rounded excursion. Hunters and anglers can make the most of their stay in New Zealand by working with experienced outfitters to maximize their chances of encountering game animals or capturing exceptional catches while complying with local restrictions and ensuring their personal safety.

Encouraging Responsible and Sustainable Practices

When it comes to hunting and fishing in New Zealand, encouraging appropriate and sustainable methods is critical. We can ensure the preservation of the country's natural resources and the integrity of its ecosystems by adopting these practices. As you set out to discover the delights of New Zealand's hunting and fishing options, please keep the following in mind:

Prioritize Conservation

Recognize the importance of maintaining the country's diverse animals and environments for future generations. Accept your responsibility as a responsible hunter or angler in preserving the fragile balance of ecosystems by following conservation rules and regulations.

Respect Wildlife

Treat wildlife with the utmost respect. Take the time to learn about the behaviors, habitats, and needs of the species you encounter. Maintain a safe distance from them to avoid disturbing or stressing them. Remember that your presence in their natural environment is a privilege, and by respecting their space, you contribute to their well-being and the health of the ecosystem as a whole.

Selective Harvesting

When hunting or fishing, use a selective method. Priority should be given to species that are plentiful and have healthy populations. When fishing, avoid taking more than you need and use catch-and-release techniques. Selective harvesting contributes to the sustainable management of populations, allowing them to thrive and ensuring the future availability of these resources.

Reliable Equipment and Techniques

Choose equipment and practices that will cause the least amount of harm to the environment and wildlife. To avoid harming fish, use a non-toxic fishing tackle and barbless hooks. Use ethical hunting equipment and tactics that ensure clean and compassionate kills. By using ethical gear and tactics, you may reduce your influence on the environment while also prioritizing the well-being of the species you encounter.

Leave No Trace

When exploring New Zealand's beautiful wilderness, remember to leave no trace. Respect the environment by disposing of waste correctly, which includes packaging, fishing lines, and other materials. Leave natural objects untouched, allowing them to contribute to the natural balance of the ecosystem. By leaving no trace, you ensure that future visitors can also experience New Zealand's natural beauty.

Promote Sustainable Tourism

Select outfitters and guides who value sustainable methods and are committed to environmental care. Support local companies and groups that work to protect New Zealand's natural resources. By partnering with sustainable tourism providers, you actively contribute to the preservation of the country's unique landscapes while also contributing to the local economy.

By embracing ethical and sustainable techniques, you not only ensure the preservation of New Zealand's natural resources, but you also enhance your personal hunting or fishing experiences. Respect wildlife, practice selective harvesting, use responsible gear, leave no trace, and advocate for sustainable tourism. Accept the opportunity to discover and experience the marvels of hunting and fishing in New Zealand with a genuine awareness of the natural world's beauty and fragility. Together, we can preserve and maintain this magnificent habitat for future generations.

Closing Remarks

Before ending the enthralling experience of hunting and fishing, take time to reflect on the incredible experiences you've endured. Reflect on how you experienced an exciting expedition in New Zealand's breathtaking landscapes, where excitement and tranquility collide to produce unforgettable moments.

From towering mountains to crystal-clear lakes and wide

coastal waters, New Zealand's natural beauties unveil themselves in all their splendor. Think about the colorful wildlife, hear rushing rivers, and experience the excitement of throwing lines into immaculate fishing holes. Immerse yourself in this gorgeous landscape, and connecting with the country's wild essence will give you immense delight.

Explore the fundamental significance of hunting and fishing in New Zealand. Discover how these activities help to conserve resources, preserve natural balance, and benefit local communities. Witness firsthand the positive influence they have on wildlife conservation, biodiversity enhancement, and guaranteeing sustainable practices for future generations.

Nevertheless, this journey isn't simply about numbers and data. It's about the intimate bonds you have formed with the land, wildlife, and traditions that make New Zealand unique. It's all about the thrill of the chase, the satisfaction of catching a valued catch, and the serenity of casting lines in the midst of a gorgeous landscape. It's about the fun you have with friends and family, the stories you tell over the campfire, and the memories you hold dear.

Set off on your own adventure into the enthralling world of New Zealand's hunting and fishing prospects and enjoy the experience with all of your senses. Allow the wind to whisper through the trees as you traverse the backcountry, the rush of the river to energize you, and the anticipation of what lies beneath the surface to fuel your excitement.

Take the time to appreciate nature's intricate beauty, respect the wildlife that lives here, and leave your own legacy of ethical and sustainable behaviors. Plunge yourself completely in this realm of adventure, and allow it to become a part of you.

With the knowledge and understanding gained from these pages, take advantage of every opportunity to explore, experience, and create your own stories in New Zealand's wilds. Whether you seek seclusion on a mountain peak or delight in the companionship of a fishing trip, may your journey be filled with wonder, discovery, and a profound connection to the extraordinary world that awaits you.

Dear reader, go forth and let the spirit of New Zealand's hunting and fishing adventures guide you to memories that will last a lifetime. This is your invitation to embrace the extraordinary, pursue your goals, and discover your place in nature's magnificent tapestry.

Thank you for coming along on this fantastic adventure. May your hunting and fishing adventures in New Zealand be filled with thrill, harmony, and the promise of innumerable unforgettable memories.

About The Author

Joshua Godfrey owns and operates an international hunting and fishing booking agency which allows him to travel all over the world on all six main continents which include the United Kingdom and New Zealand. He is an Author of the Head Hunters-Hunting Safaris Around The Globe Series.

Printed in Great Britain
by Amazon